Middle Eastern Cooking

Christine Osborne

PRION

Contents

Foreword   6

Introduction   8

Mezze   20

Soups   42

Salads   54

Vegetables and Rice   66

Seafood   80

Meat   92

Poultry   110

Desserts and Sweetmeats   124

Drinks   140

Index   150

Acknowledgements   152

TOP LEFT
Ripening dates in the Shatt el-Arab delta, southern Iraq.
TOP RIGHT
Boxed fruits from the West Bank of the river Jordan.
BOTTOM LEFT
Mezze *as it is served in a Beirut restaurant.*
BOTTOM RIGHT
Spices for sale in a spice market in downtown Amman.

A Bedouin pounding coffee beans in southern Jordan. Coffee is drunk at every opportunity throughout the Middle East.

Foreword

As you might imagine, I had many adventures in my endeavours to learn the secrets of Middle Eastern cooking.

Most unusual was a lunch in north Yemen in a restaurant no bigger than a large hole in the wall. This is precisely what it was, a cavity in the wall around the capital, Sana'a, into which an enterprising Yemeni had manoeuvered some tables and chairs.

I had not finished eating when the space was invaded by crowds of men who, unable to squeeze past, walked across the top of my table. Then, finding a seat, they unclipped daggers and hung them on a hook as a westerner might his umbrella. No one paid me, the only woman, the slightest attention. As far as they knew, I might have been a *djinn!* *

Quite the opposite was a lavish banquet in Saudi Arabia in honour of the visit by Her Majesty Queen Elizabeth II and the Duke of Edinburgh.

All that day refrigerated vans had sped the best of Arab and imported delicacies between Riyadh, the Saudi capital, and a spot in the desert, marked by a mammoth tent. Lobster had been flown in from Jeddah, and truffles from France, and fifty lambs had been slaughtered for the occasion, which was to be attended by hundreds of sheikhs. The hospitable Saudis had even extended the invitation to include the press – an unheard-of event in royal circles – which was how I found myself dining with the Queen, Her Majesty being obscured, however, by pyramids of dates.

Between these two remarkable occasions lie a wealth of memories and a host of meals – many of which are recaptured in *Middle Eastern Cooking.*

Western interest in Middle Eastern cooking is part of the general trend towards trying out new foods. First introduced to Chinese and Indian cooking and more recently to Japanese and Thai, people are now curious about ethnic cooking in general.

An interest in Levantine cuisine grew from contact with Lebanese uprooted by years of war. Fleeing abroad many subsequently opened restaurants and sweetmeats shops so that today you can eat Middle Eastern food in almost any big city in the west. London, Paris and Sydney in particular have large Lebanese communities and a buoyant restaurant trade.

Oil rich Arabs travelling abroad also brought their own cooks to prepare meals according to Muslim dietary laws. Before long hotels in places patronised by Arabs began employing their own Muslim chefs, exposing westerners to Middle Eastern cooking.

Tour groups returning from Turkey and Jordan, business travellers from the Arab states and expatriates returning from employment in Iran and Iraq also enthused about the local cuisine. In consequence there is a great interest in regional dishes although most overseas restaurants generally limit their menus to a few assuredly popular dishes. So the only way to sample true ethnic cooking is to prepare it yourself from a traditional recipe at home.

Other recipes are missing for obvious reasons. It is not feasible to try smoking Iraqi *mashgouf* around a fire in your kitchen. Nor to cook *khouzi*, an Arab recipe requiring a whole sheep. Without help, sweetmeats such as *knaffeh* and Turkish Delight are very time-consuming to prepare. Today's Middle Eastern housewife usually buys them ready made.

Bread is also frequently purchased from the baker who makes several batches throughout the day. Many breads are too big to bake in a domestic oven and are cooked in a large, beehive-shaped oven or *tanour*. Similar types are sold in Lebanese and Turkish food shops or failing this, the Greek *pitta* and Indian *naan* are similar. On a recent visit to Sydney I discovered *khoubz* in a supermarket.

A resident of London, but born in Australia, I was brought up on beef, but my taste has changed radically after extensive travels in the Middle East – today I do not eat beef at all preferring seafood to anything else.

My own interest in Middle Eastern food developed following an initial visit to Lebanon, the heartland of Middle Eastern cooking, in 1971. Similar to any other western visitor, I was eager to acquire some regional recipes to entertain at home. I did not want anything too elaborate, since like most working women, cooking time is limited to weekends, but I sought some easily prepared dishes for entertaining on busy week nights.

I trust the same applies to you and that *Middle Eastern Cooking* will bring new pleasures to your table. *Bismillah!* **

CHRISTINE OSBORNE

djinn a spirit in Muslim mythology
**Bismillah!* (in the name of God!), as expressed by an Arab before eating.

Introduction

Media coverage of the seventeen-year-long civil war in Lebanon and the more recent Gulf War give the impression that the Middle East is a land of blazing guns. Yet the millions of citizens going to work in Cairo or Ankara, or the *felaheen* (farmers) toiling in the fields, represent a far more accurate picture of daily life.

The belly of the Orient, the Middle East sweeps east from Egypt through the countries of the Fertile Crescent as far as Iran and encompasses the vast land mass of the Arabian peninsula. The majority of people speak Arabic and share a common heritage with colourful regional variations in music, costume and cuisine.

While parts of the Middle East are largely desert, elsewhere is as green as the Cotswolds, as the name, the Fertile Crescent, implies. Other areas are even subtropical like the beautiful palm-fringed coast of Dhofar, in southern Oman. Between these extremes is a rugged mix of pebble plains and dunes where Bedouin nomads still migrate from oasis to oasis.

According to archaeologists and historians, civilization in the Middle East began sometime in the fifth millennium BC in Mesopotamia.

We know little about the diet of the ancient peoples but it seems likely that they had the same pulse-based dishes as the *felaheen* of today, and because the region was rich in wildlife, game birds, gazelle and wild boar were probably popular.

Ancient civilizations and conquering armies have bequeathed to the Middle East a rich architectural heritage: the remains of giant dams, soaring pyramids, and magical-sounding cities such as Persepolis and Petra. In the absence of records, one can only assume that peoples of such building expertise also possessed sophisticated culinary skills.

The expansion of the Greek and Roman empires undoubtedly contributed to the cuisine in the Middle East, and the spread of Islam from Arabia introduced humble but wholesome foods.

Ruling from Baghdad, the Abbasid dynasty (AD 750–1258) is known to have been passionately interested in cooking. Many popular present-day recipes have origins in Abbasid kitchens.

The Ottoman Empire introduced the stuffed vegetable dishes so popular in Middle Eastern cookery. British and French mandates following the First World War also added new ideas, but by then Middle Eastern cooking styles were firmly established and while western dishes were applauded, local habits remained unchanged.

The amalgam of so many cuisines makes Middle Eastern food unique and at the same time difficult to define. Basically it can be described as wholesome and well flavoured, spicy without being fiery hot, and notable for several items in particular: *mezze* or starters, stuffed vegetables and meats, and rich sweetmeats. It is not merely the food, however, that anks Middle Eastern cooking – not before time – with the world's greatest cuisines, but its presentation and the surroundings in which it is served.

REGIONAL COOKING - THE LEVANT
While Middle Eastern cooking follows a basic theme, there are regional variations: Levantines eat more grilled meat and yogurt than, say, the Yemenis; Yemenis, on the other hand, like spicy dishes; Persian recipes dabble in a subtle combination of fruit and meat; curries have crept into the Arab cuisine, and so on. There is little difference in etiquette except where contact with the West has influenced customs.

The countries of the eastern Mediterranean littoral, or the Levant – Lebanon, Syria and Jordan – enjoy a similar cuisine; however the same dish may be called by different names, which is rather confusing, in the same way that cooking methods – a pinch of this, or a handful of that – are often vague. Of the three cuisines, Jordanian cooking is most basic, a mix of Bedouin food from the eastern desert and warming dishes from the western escarpment. Syrian cooking tends to be more elaborate, while the best known, Lebanese, is noted for the stylish presentation of food and the infinite variety of dishes.

The flavours of Lebanon are those most commonly associated with Middle Eastern cookery: the tangy taste of chopped mint, garlic and lemon juice in an olive oil dressing; the smoky taste of purées made from roasted sesame seeds and grilled aubergines; the subtle taste of rose water in desserts. While the aroma of Turkish coffee percolates the entire Middle East, this too is unmistakably Lebanese.

If any race lives to eat, it is the affable Lebanese; a nation of shrewd entrepreneurs who find any excuse a good reason to mix business with the pleasure of eating. In Arabic, the word *lebnan* is derived from an

BELOW *Scales fly off a fine bream
in Muscat, Sultanate of Oman.
The Omanis are great fish-eaters.*
RIGHT *A farmer's wife sifting
through pulses before making a
soup in Upper Egypt.*

Aramaic word meaning white, a reference to the snow-covered mountains behind Beirut, but also to *laban*, which in Lebanon means curdled milk, a dish of thick, creamy yogurt being a popular *mezze*.

Mezze or starters are the best-known aspect of Lebanese cuisine. They consist of many small dishes, either true *hors d'oeuvre* or miniature main courses, laid out for people to serve themselves as in a Scandinavian *smörgasbord*. Some of the endless *mezze* recipes are described in the first chapter.

A typical meal may consist solely of *mezze* or have several courses, such as stuffed meat and vegetable dishes, *kebabs*, a fish or poultry dish, salads and rice, ending with fresh fruit, sweetmeats and coffee. A water pipe, or *nargila*, may be brought in for the

men, its gentle bubbling adding to the convivial atmosphere. *Arak* is commonly drunk with a *mezze*. Lebanon also produces some of the best wines in the Middle East. The Lebanese particularly like eating out of doors, it being debatable whether they, or the Turks, invented the custom of *al fresco* dining.

Syrian food is equally appetizing with a fondness of *mezze* shared with the Lebanese. *Bulghur* is widely used in cooking and Syrian housewives are reputedly the best *kibbeh* makers in the Middle East. Seafood is available on the Mediterranean coast.

Part of the Fertile Crescent, Syria is self-sufficient in vegetables and fruits – pears, grapes and delicious figs. Preserved apricots are a speciality of Damascus. Together with almonds and walnuts, pistachio nuts are

BELOW *A Bedouin woman making buttermilk the traditional way in Dubai. She will sit and shake the liquid all day.*
RIGHT *In from the country, an old man shopping in a Jerusalem souk.*

used in the sweetmeats, at which Syrian pastry bakers excel. Aleppo is renowned for superb pastries and rich desserts.

Syria produces similar fruity wines to the Lebanon. *Arak* is drunk with *mezze*. Traditional fruit juices – tamarind, orange and pomegranate – are losing ground to bottled soft drinks. Tea is drunk at every opportunity. Coffee is always served with a large glass of water to quench the thirst. Yogurt-and-water is drunk by the Bedouin.

Several Jordanian dishes have roots in Bedouin cooking. The best example is *mansaf*, meaning "the large tray" or dish on which this traditional repast is served. A vast communal dinner, *mansaf* consists of slices of stewed mutton, rice, bread and *jameed* (a

dried sheep's milk yogurt crumbled, melted and poured over the food). Similar to the Arab *khouzi*, *mansaf* is served on the floor of a tent with everyone sitting around the dish helping themselves.

Fatir is a popular people's food, consisting of unleavened bread soaked in yogurt and topped with *samneh* (or clarified butter).

In Amman *mezze* are popular: variations are *kishki*, or yogurt mixed with chopped walnuts and olive oil and sprinkled with the lemony spice known as *sumak*. Most *mezze* are an extension of Lebanese cuisine.

Soups are not widespread, perhaps because of the rich sauces that accompany many main courses. Soups made from lentils, meat and vegetables and *frieka* (cracked smoked wheat) are most common, especially in the westen escarpment overlooking the Dead Sea.

Popular main courses are: *yakneh* (a meat and vegetable casserole), *mahshi* or stuffed vegetables, chicken and *kebabs*. *Shawarma* (sliced lamb on a skewer) is as popular in Jordan as it is in Syria or Lebanon.

Like poultry, meat is marinated to tenderize and to absorb flavours. A common custom adds coriander fried with garlic to many recipes: a small wooden pestle and mortar used solely for grinding this mixture is kept in every kitchen. Common vegetables in Jordanian cooking are tomatoes, okra, cabbage and aubergines. Rice is more popular as a side dish there than in Syria or Lebanon, a custom linked to basic Bedouin cooking.

Shops in America specialize in *knaffeh*, a cream cheese sweetmeat with Palestinian origins. Most local sweetmeats are made throughout the Levant.

Bread is eaten with every meal with many variations on the common, rounded unleavened pocket bread known simply as a *khoubz*. People buy *ka'ik bil sim-sim*, a soft bread ring sprinkled with sesame seeds that is sold with a boiled egg and a tiny packet of spices, to eat on their way to work.

TURKEY

Ottoman domination of the Middle East had a big influence on ethnic cooking. Many recipes have Turkish origins: who but the Turks would call dishes "Dainty Fingers" or "Lady's Thighs" – *kadin budu*?

The Ottoman sultans' opulent tastes also extended to the kitchen. The largest parts of the Topkapi Palace were the kitchens, where we are told that some sixty chefs and two hundred assistants devised special delicacies. It is said they had at least forty ways of cooking aubergine and more than sixty ways of making *baklava*. There were specialists for *böreks* (stuffed pastries), cooks for fish, meat and poultry, and makers of sweetmeats.

Based on meat and dairy products, Turkish food is high in protein. Plain yogurt is greatly enjoyed, blended into soups and sauces, or as a flavour in cakes. White cheese is always found in a *meze* (*mezze*) with other starters.

Seafood is popular on the coast, while lamb is the basic meat. The *döner kebap* (turning kebab) has travelled to the far corners of the earth with Turkish migrants. *Döner kebap* (*shawarma* in Arabic) slowly turning on a skewer is a familiar sight. Pieces of lamb are loaded on to a vertical skewer which slowly turns in front of an electric grill. As they cook, they are sliced off into a tray, or if a customer is waiting, into a pocket of *ekmek* (pitta bread) which is filled with salad.

Turkish cooks perform miracles with the most mundane vegetables. Plain by most standards, the cabbage is elevated to regal status by stuffing it with rice, raisins and pine nuts. The stuffed aubergine dish *Imam bayildi* (swooning Imam) has captured the imagination of cooks all over the world. Rice is habitually served with main courses; Turks like long-grain rice cooked so that a little moisture remains.

Desserts are those based on milk, such as *muhallabia*, or rice pudding, and those made from pastry such as *baklava*. The most famous sweetmeat is *lokum*, known popularly as "Turkish Delight".

Traditional beverages are beer, wine and *raki* (arak). Made from grapes and aniseed, *raki* clouds when water is added giving it the popular name of *Aslan sutu* or "lion's milk". Other drinks are *aryan* (yogurt and water) and *shira* or grape juice. Turkish coffee is served *Sekersiz* (without surgar), *orta sekerli* (medium) or *serkerli* (plenty of sugar).

EGYPT

To know what foods were most prized by the ancient Egyptians we are indebted to their murals and bas-reliefs. Paintings adorning the Tombs of the Nobles in Luxor and carvings on the temple erected to Hathor, the Cow Goddess worshipped in Dendera, and on other monuments at Edfu and Kom Ombo on the Upper Nile are subjects bearing gifts of ducks, fish, wheat, grapes and jars of honey.

The foods still enjoyed in Egypt have in essence changed little. Small farms in the belt of irrigated land along the Nile grow wheat, okra, chick-peas, beans and the spinach-like vegetable base of *melokhia*, a soup which enjoyed widespread popularity in Pharoanic times. Ducks are kept by every rural family, pigeons flutter in and out of lofts, water buffalo provide rich, creamy milk and in villages all over Egypt women continue to bake unleavened bread in dome-shaped ovens that were in vogue 3000 years ago. But unless it is the delicious tasting *melokhia*, Egypt cannot really be said to have a national dish. The wholesome food tends to be unexciting when compared to the refined cuisine of the Levant which lends recipes such as *babaghannouj* and *knaffeh* to the local repertoire.

Early risers in any town will find the souqs already crowded with people clamouring to buy the soft, round *baladi* bread which is eaten with *foule*, a brown bean puree, as a substantial breakfast. Still others queue in front of the *falafel* stands preparing ground white bean rissoles which are fried and eaten dipped in *tahini*.

Poultry is greatly prized. Similar to meat, it is usually eaten with potato chips, or short grain rice cultivated in the lush Nile delta. Many *felaheen* (farmers) keep pigeons for their eggs and to fatten for the pot. Poultry is normally grilled or cooked on a rotisserie. A more elaborate recipe for Nubian chicken requires a chicken leg to be stuffed with rice and chopped tomato and liver to which a generous pinch of cinnamon is added. This popular dish from Upper Egypt is then baked in an oven.

Lamb is the meat of choice with locally reared, non-fatty lamb being preferred to imported mutton. Char-grilled lamb kebabs, *shawarma*, and leg of lamb stewed with vegetables are common ways of preparation. *Fatta*, chopped and simmered lamb using bread to mop up the unctuous stock, is often made when many guests are expected. A generous pinch of pepper, paprika and cumin is added to heighten the flavour.

Red Sea fish such as mullet, cod and various reef fish, usually grilled or cooked as kebabs, are widely eaten by the coastal communities. While the great Nile river yields several varieties of fish for millions of *felaheen* living along its banks. *Bolty*, a member of the perch family, and *karmoot* (catfish) are popular freshwater fish either fried or grilled.

Poor families may only eat from the abundance of sun ripened vegetables grown in Egypt. A wander through any souq reveals piles of glossy purple eggplants, heaps of emerald green courgettes and mountains of blush red tomatoes. *Bamia* (okra) is very popular in a stew with mutton or an ingredient in a vegetable casserole.

Fruits round off a meal, commonly bananas, oranges and dates but also locally grown grapes, guavas and pomegranates. Sweetmeats such as *knaffeh, basbousa*

and *lokum* are served on special occasions. The delightfully named *Umm Ali* (Ali's Mother) is a wonderful, creamy pudding with origins in Mughal cuisine.

Tea brewed very strong using lots of sugar is the most popular beverage in Egypt. On every street is a tea-house filled with men drinking little glasses of black tea while smoking a *shisha* or water pipe and enjoying a game of dominoes. Fresh orange juice, sugar-cane juice and mineral water are other thirst quenchers. Local wines while not highly rated are drunk by the middle class.

THE ARAB STATES

With the exceptions of Yemen and the Sultanate of Oman which warrant individual entries cooking throughout the vast Arabian peninsula is basically quite similar. Before wealth from oil enabled them to import foodstuffs and to acquire farming expertize, a majority of Arabs lived on a rugged diet of bread, rice, dates and whatever meat was available. People living on the Gulf coast and along the Red Sea also had access to seafood. A map of the Arabian Gulf drawn by the renowned Egyptian geographer Ptolemy in 150 AD even refers to the Lower Gulf, the region now known as the United Arab Emirates, by the Greek *Icthyophagi*, "fish-eaters".

A traditional culinary event ever popular is the *khouzi*. In essence the national dish of Arabia, it is prepared on occasions of special significance: a tribal marriage, or a religious feast day such as *Eid el fitr*, the celebration which follows the fasting of Ramadan. It consists of an entire sheep, or a young camel cooked for many hours in an underground pit. When tender, dried yoghurt is crumbled, melted and poured over the sliced meat arranged on a bed of rice to which pine nuts, raisins and saffron have been added. Seated on a carpet around the platter of food, diners help themselves using unleavened bread to soak up the juices.

Seafood remains a highlight of regional cuisine with the local fish markets becoming tourist attractions. Dubai, Abu Dhabi, Kuwait and Jeddah on the Red Sea littoral all have vibrant souqs selling scores of different reef and open water fish. *Hamour* (cod) and *Sultan Ibrahim*, the rather grand local name for Red Mullet are the most popular. A traditional way of cooking fish

An elaborate table setting during Eid al-fitr, the holiday following Ramadan, the month of fasting.

Among themselves, most Arab families eat off a cloth spread on the living room floor. However, if a western guest is present, a table will be set with crockery and cutlery.

uses a dome-shaped barbecue with glowing coals at the base. The fish is cooked on skewers with the stick passed in through the mouth. Stuffing and baking is another common method of preparing a good plump fish among which *chanad* and *zubaidi* are other popular species. Red Sea prawns and *Umm Robien*, a flat, Scyllarid lobster are eaten simply grilled adding a squeeze of Batinah lime or *loomi*.

Many of the Arab states from once having only grown dates and limes are today self sufficient in basic foodstuffs including vegetables, poultry and eggs. Saudi Arabia and Abu Dhabi have been especially successful in growing eggplants, beans, marrows, cabbages, courgettes and the long green cucumbers called *trooh*. Tomatoes cultivated in the pollution free conditions in the desert taste as sweet as strawberries.

A fruit salad is likely to consist of locally grown strawberries and tropical fruits. Bananas, pineapples, guavas and mangoes are cultivated in the wetter region of south-west Arabia, even apples on Sir Bani Yas, a private island with a cooler climate lying out in the Arabian Gulf. And with strawberries grown in Sharjah, you can add cream produced by dairy herds in Ras al Khaimah whose micro-climate also grows 60 per cent of vegetables in the Emirates.

Lebanese *mezze* have been adopted as starters to a majority of meals if not at home, then certainly by the hotels. Many – the Gulf Hotel in Doha, the Safir International in Kuwait and the Hyatt Regency in Dubai being especially recommended – prepare a Middle Eastern buffet lunch for guests. *Hummus, babaghanouj, tabbouleh* and stuffed vine leaves are among the fifteen to twenty most common appetisers.

Traditional *shawarma*, sliced, skewered meat cooked on a rotisserie, still holds out against the Fast Food restaurants opening up in all the Arab capitals – at last count, Kuwait City, as an example, a dozen Kentucky Fried Chicken outlets. Barbecued chicken is a common Arab dish but the chicken *biryani* sold in hundreds of eateries is of Indian, not Arab origin.

The subtle use of herbs and spices is a feature of Middle Eastern recipes. Many are native to the region, but widely available in the West.

Khoubz, flat, unleavened bread comes in several varieties but the ingredients and cooking methods have changed little over thousands of years. Wheat flour and barley flour remain popular but corn flour is increasingly used.

Puddings and sweetmeats in Arabia are those common to the rest of the Middle East: *muhallabia*, *Umm Ali* and sticky honey and nut pastries such as *baklava*. Saffron rice with raisins, pine nuts and a drop or two of rosewater is also popular.

Baharat, a flavoursome ingredient mixed from half a dozen spices usually including nutmeg, paprika, cumin and cardamon, is prepared to individual taste and widely used to flavour soup, poultry and fish

dishes. Turmeric and saffron are used to colour foods especially fish and rice.

Mineral water is by and large the most popular beverage throughout the Arab world followed by blender-mixed fruit-juice cocktails. *Qahwa* is a pale lemon coloured, bitter tasting brew made from cardamon husks and served at every opportunity. Turkish coffee is also popular.

SULTANATE OF OMAN
Traditional Omani cuisine is unknown outside this ruggedly beautiful country on the south-east shores of Arabia. Even within Oman it is hard to find authentic cooking outside a private home. Only one restaurant –

the *Al Aqur* in Nizwa serves local dishes combining savoury, sweet and spicy flavours designed to tantalize the palate.

Delicious, innovative and eclectic, Omani cooking is an amalgam of many different foods introduced through cosmopolitan trade links dating back hundreds of years. Sailors and merchants returning from India, Zanzibar and East African ports brought home new tastes and exotic spices which were eventually absorbed into the local repertoire.

Cooking on the coast is more experimental. The interior is cut off by mountain ranges and the recipes are purer Omani in concept but there are regional variations. Dhofar in the south has been influenced by the African tastes of a large population of former slaves. Exotic fish recipes dominate in the barren Sharqiya while *biryani*-type dishes prevail in the Musandam peninsula, only a day's voyage by dhow to Pakistan.

A meal in Oman frequently starts with a bowl of soup. The most common soups are based on grains – wheat, oats, barley and lentils – but meat or chicken and vermicelli soup are equally popular. People of the Sharqiya have an almost Oriental fondness for *awal*, (shark's fin soup).

Main courses are based on meat, fish and poultry. Goat is a favourite, Omanis have a recipe for every part of the animal including the guts. *Muqalab* is a delicious garlic and clove flavoured tripe casserole popular in the Muscat governorate. *Marak al qeema*, a mildly sweet mince curry shows an Indian influence. In Dhofar the recipe for *al majeen* involves frying boneless beef or camel, cooling it and serving it with dates. Widely eaten as a breakfast during Ramadan, *harees* is meat pounded into a paste and boiled very slowly with wheat, cardamon and other spices. *Bizar* – an all-spice comprising pepper, coriander, cumin, cardamon, cinnamon, nutmeg, ginger and cloves – is a common ingredient.

If there are three hundred ways of preparing chicken in the Middle East, Oman counts at least the same number of ways for cooking fish with a recipe for everything from the benevolent Arabian Sea. Additives to fish stews include coconut milk, fresh tomato puree, onions, garlic, tamarind, paprika and limes. *Al ouwidat*, fish balls rolled in chick-pea flour, made chilli hot is a speciality of the northern Batinah coast. By contrast to the popularity of fish, Omanis do

not much care for crustacea such as lobster and abalone.

A vegetable dish as well as a salad is always served with the main course which may comprise of two, or three different dishes. Variations of plain *kabuli* rice include rice with meat cubes, chick peas, onions, cloves and raisins. Rice is boiled or fried in ghee – Omanis do not cook in oil.

Bread is used to mop up the juices and although bakers tend only to cook one type of plain, unleavened wheat flour bread, there are more than 20-30 different variations on this theme. *Khoubz rakhal* is a thin, almost translucent bread cooked early to eat after prayers. *Khoubz al sim sim* is sesame seed bread, *khoubz tawa* date bread and *khoubz al mouz* banana bread.

Halwa is a favourite sweetmeat based on sugar and rosewater and made in huge tubs in the souqs. Other sticky sweetmeats include coconut and dates. Desserts such as *siwaya bil haleeb*, baked vermicelli and milk garnished with almonds and pistacchio nuts, and the creamy *al firni* have Mughal links. Dates from Oman's estimated 10 million palms are always passed around at the end of a meal.

Black tea drunk with lots of sugar is the most popular beverage. Omanis also like ginger, mint, lemon and cinnamon teas.

Many of these dishes and other more *outre* items such as locust broth can be sampled at *Al Aqur*.

YEMEN
Traditional Yemeni food is unknown outside Yemen, a raggedly beautiful country with the most spectacular domestic architecture in the Middle Ages.

Local diet is based on several highly original dishes that can be attributed to the country's long isolation. Others show an Ottoman influence, while a taste for spicy foods results from contact with Indian traders on the Tihama or Red Sea coast.

Food is always fresh. No Yemeni housewife would dream of dishing up leftovers; what is not eaten is distributed among the less fortunate. A negative side is that most dishes are served boiling hot and thus lose their nutritional value. Due to economic restraints, few dishes are very nourishing and the truly unique Yemeni recipes are unlikely to appeal to a western palate. Others common to Middle Eastern cookery –

such as lentil soup and okra stew – appear in this book.

Bread is the basis of every meal; the most common is a round, unleavened bread baked from sorghum flour, which is ground by the housewife or taken to the local miller. *Bint al sahin* is a cross between bread and a pudding, eaten hot as a savoury dish or smothered with *samneh* and honey.

Sheep's or goats' milk is soured by prolonged vigorous shaking in a gourd, the resultant buttermilk being used in the preparation of many dishes. Farmers in the Tihama foothills make a first-class smoked goats' milk cheese, known as *jubn*, which is sold in Ta'iz, the old capital.

Soups are popular, especially in the cooler highlands. The most common is *helba*, based on ground fenugreek seeds which are whipped to a froth, with meat stock, hot pepper and other seasonings.

Similar to the Levant, dips are a tradition, but in Yemen they are different. *Zahawiq*, the best known, is made from tomatoes and chilli to which tiny dried fish are sometimes added. *Foul* is eaten daily. Other pulses are made into stews. *Asid* is a thick gruel-like porridge made from sorghum, boiling water, oil and honey or broth. Mutton is the most common meat, the brain and liver being especially revered.

Most days Yemenis forego breakfast in favour of a large lunch before the *qat*-chewing session. Chewed every afternoon, the leaf depresses the appetite, supper in consequence being late and light. On market day, breakfast is a tradition for farmers who travel long distances. Typical breakfasts are chick peas served with fried liver, *fattah* (a dough made from dates, bananas and butter) and *mattit* (egg, tomatoes, peppers and onions made into a soup mixed with crumbled bread, butter and honey).

Most foods are cooked in vegetable oils. *Alya*, lard obtained from the melted down fatty tail of sheep, is popular in rural areas. Cooking facilities remain primitive; most women cook over a fire in the kitchen, or at the entrance to their house. When something special is made, it is a custom to send a portion to a neighbour.

When the meal is ready, everyone sits around the cloth, unless strangers are present, in which case women eat separately. Traditionally served first, men receive the choicest portions of food (a custom throughout the entire Middle East).

A meal is eaten in a special order. The first course is white radish, which is dipped in *helba*. A salad follows, with *bint al sahin*, soup and hot vegetable dishes such as okra and potatoes. The last course is usually mutton stew, or grilled chicken with rice. This menu is typical of a middle-class urban family; most Yemenis eat a lot less.

Special foods are eaten during the fast of Ramadan. Similar to other countries in the Middle East, the fast is broken with dates, grapes and other fruits, followed by a large meal. In the mountains, soups replace gruel, while *muhallabia* is a popular Ramadan dessert.

IRAN

Iranian, or Persian cooking is very sophisticated, a fact not generally appreciated ouside the country. While Iran benefits from being largely agricultural, local recipes display real genius in combining many unusual ingredients in particular the sweet and sour flavours of *polou*, a casserole, featuring exotic fruits such as peaches, pomegranates and cherries.

Bread is served with every meal and still traditionally baked in a bee-hive shaped clay *tannour* oven. *Sangyak* is a crisp uneven, flat bread, *taftoon* is round and made with wholemeal flour while *barbari*, a popular breakfast bread baked from white flour is more than 60cm (24 inches) long.

Most meals in Iran start with a soup or *borani*, a salad, usually of spinach or cucumber and lettuce with raisins served on a thick base of creamy yoghurt. *Pish ghaza*, appetisers similar to *mezze* are prepared on special occasions with as many as forty small dishes set out on the buffet table.

Main courses include a variety of mutton and poultry dishes, usually roasted or stewed with the addition of herbs and spices. Cooked slowly, the sauce, *khoresh*, becomes rich and aromatic and is poured over rice and eaten as a substantial meal.

Chelo kebab is the most famous dish in the Persian kitchen. The best cuts of lamb are thinly sliced and marinated with diced onion and lemon juice. After cooking briefly on hot coals, the meat is arranged on a cushion of puffy white rice. Dabs of butter and a raw yolk of egg are mixed into the rice and *sumak*, a pink, lemony tasting spice, is sprinkled on top. Slivers of onion, radishes and a sprig of parsley act as a garnish. A queue outside a restaurant indicates a good *chelo kebab* is served inside.

In Iran rice is the most important element in any dish and when cooked well, it has no equal. Popular are steamed rice, *chelo*, and *katteh*, a moulded rice served in wedges. Local rice is very hard-grained, but Basmati rice can be used as a suitable substitute.

The Iranian caviar fishing industry is centred in Babolsar on the Caspian Sea. The grey-green beluga caviar from the elephant sturgeon is the best quality. Sturgeon themselves are a great delicacy. The thick fillets are lightly smoked and served poached with a green lemon juice dressing. Rural restaurants serve grilled trout, while the Gulf cities enjoy good seafood in common with most Arab countries.

Desserts tend to be either rather heavy or very sweet, a general trend throughout the Middle East. Stuffed apples and quinces are very popular.

The country produces an abundance of fruits – oranges, peaches, pomegranates and watermelons from the Isfahan Oasis. Many fruits are made into *sharbats* – from which the word sorbet derives.

Extolled by Farsi poets, Persian wine was of considerable quality, one of the main wine-growing regions being around Shiraz, "the city of wine and roses". *Abdug* or yogurt-and-water is drunk during a meal. People drink tea rather than coffee and no self-respecting household is without a samovar.

IRAQ

The art of Middle Eastern cookery reached its zenith during the Abbasid era in Baghdad – the city of Sheherezade and tales from "A Thousand and One Nights".

The culinary skills of Abbasid chefs were renowned: great chefs were presented at court, the lavishness of their creations was extolled by poets, and lengthy treaties were written on the noble are of cookery. Ancient cookery manuals refer to banquets lasting for days, with table after table laden with roast partridges, ducks and francolins that had been marinated overnight in curd; milk-fed kid and spitted gazelle, and platters of sweetmeats.

With the exception of one or two regional dishes, Iraqi cooking follows general trends with an historic Persian bias. While most Iraqis eat sparingly, when they do eat, it resembles a last supper. An Iraqi dining table is invariably loaded with exotic foods.

An elaborate silver tamarind juice stand in Damascus, Syria.

Starters are usually stuffed potatoes, *dolmas* and salads. Spiked with mint, yogurt is popular, while rice dishes are similar to Persian varieties. The most elaborate, *timman za'fran*, includes minced meat, raisins and nuts – a substantial meal.

A variation on the famous Saudi *khouzi* steams a whole lamb on a domestic stove, then barbecues it over a bed of rice in a *tanour*. Suspended head down, the fatty tail constantly bastes the carcass as it melts.

Parks and gardens line the Tigris River flowing through Baghdad, where restaurants are set out under the trees. A traditional dish is *mashgouf*, a delicious fish which is slowly smoked around an open fire and served with sliced tomatoes, onions and bread.

Fish and dates are twin products in Basra, at the head of the Arabian Gulf. Dates have a myriad uses – barbecued fish with date purée is typical of Basra, dates are made into *halwa*, a toffee-like sweet, and stuffed in pastries.

Mentioned in the *Arabian Nights*, the sweet, orange-coloured rosettes known as *zlabiya* are still popular. Sweetmeats and coffee are served in the living room. If people have used their fingers to eat, a servant may bring a jug of water and soap to wash. Most urban houses have western-style bathrooms.

A village baker and his young sister in Iran. The huge, long loaves of bread hang outside his bakery.

ETIQUETTE, CUSTOMS AND COOKING TIPS

Living an isolated existence in the desert, Bedouin nomads display the same characteristics as an American family in the Midwest, or Australians in the Outback. Hospitality is second nature: while having no idea from where their next meal may come, they will offer what they have – their last bread or dates. In extending their hospitality, reflected in the coffee ceremony (see pages 141 to 147), they consider it their duty to protect a guest, even a complete stranger. As more and more Bedouin exchange nomadism for a sedentary life, these same unwritten rules apply in the city.

There are certain rules of etiquette in the Middle East which *Orientales*, as people refer to themselves, have observed since the revelations of the holy *Quran*. "Cleanliness is next to godliness" is a saying that may have come from Muslim society. It is unthinkable not to wash before saying one's prayers, or sitting down to eat. Even basic Arab restaurants have a corner basin. Incense is frequently burned to purify the air.

A strict code of etiquette as mealtimes expresses subtle distinctions among the diners. An important guest will be offered special delicacies such as the tail of the chicken, and so on. The host has the first taste, a custom to show the food is worthy of being eaten and to encourage others to eat.

A meal always commences with thanks to Allah, the provider – *bismillah*! Morsels of food are taken or accepted using only the right hand. One should never refuse pieces offered by one's host as it is considered impolite. If seated on the floor, the soles of one's feet must not be displayed as this, too, is considered ill-mannered. Other aspects of local etiquette are similar to western table manners: not to fill one's mouth too full, not to finish eating in order not to embarrass others.

DIETARY LAWS

Muslim dietary laws are prescribed in the *Quran*, the book of revelations revealed to the Prophet Muhammed by the Angel Gabriel in seventh-century Arabia and later transcribed by his companions.

Food is frequently mentioned, the major rules being abstention from eating the flesh of swine, the blood of any animal, or indeed eating any animal that has not been slaughtered in the correct manner by a Muslim (*hilal*). Muslims slit the throat of a beast, at the same time repeating the phrase: "In the name of God, God is most great!" Alcoholic drinks are forbidden.

SPICES

Middle Eastern food is characterized by the subtle use of spices bought in the *attarine* or spice street, where traders squat in tiny shops among boxes of colourful spices.

While today the emphasis is on the value of spices as flavourings, they have always had uses as homeopathic remedies, as vegetable dyes and in purification rituals.

Cassia and cinnamon were essential components in Egyptian embalming oils. Frankincense and cinnamon were among the gifts taken by the Queen of Sheba on her historic journey to Jerusalem. Frankincense and myrrh were also offered to the infant Jesus in Bethlehem.

Contact with the East inevitably introduced spices to western kitchens: crusading knights brought new ideas for flavourings; and the use of spices in Abbasid society was second to none.

The following spices are commonly used in Middle Eastern cooking:

A native of the Middle East, anise is cultivated for its small, oil-bearing seeds. Allspice is a fragrant spice, like a blend of cinnamon, nutmeg and cloves. It is used in stuffings.

The Middle East is the world's biggest importer of cardamon, whose crushed seeds are blended with meat dishes, while whole pods flavour desserts and coffee.

While paprika is used in many regions, hotter spices such as chilli powder are generally restricted to the Yemen. Cinnamon is used in a variety of dishes, while cloves are used to flavour veal and other dishes. Coriander is another native spice, which Mesopotamian records claim was cultivated in the fabled hanging gardens of Babylon.

Cumins, the "queen of spices", is also a native of the Middle East. Its delicate aroma complements many vegetable dishes and salads – *falafel* need a good pinch of cumin to enliven their flavour. Used ground or whole, cumin is an ingredient in Gulf fish curries. Ground fenugreek seeds help thicken curries and are excellent served with potatoes and aubergines.

Ginger appears in many medieval recipes, its medicinal value being noted in the *Quran*. Ginger tea is a soothing beverage. Abbasid society used nutmeg as a remedy for intestinal disorders; today it is used as a flavour and decoration for desserts.

The world's most popular spice, pepper is used to flavour savoury dishes, and if pepper tops the popularity poll, then saffron is the world's most expensive spice. It requires over 250,000 crocus stigmas to make a pound of saffron but only a few strands to give a beautiful glow to rice and poultry dishes. Turmeric, a yellow Indian spice, is a cheaper alternative, but no substitute in terms of flavour.

Sesame seed is historically a valuable spice in the Middle East. Raw or roasted, its seeds flavour many dishes and breads. Sesame seed oil is used on salads and in cooking.

FESTIVALS

There are several important religious festivals in the Muslim calendar.

Eid al-fitr is observed in the tenth month, following Ramadan, the month of fasting, when fasting from dawn until dusk is considered good self-discipline and spiritually uplifting. It begins when the new moon is sighted over Mecca, in Saudi Arabia. Special sweets are made for the celebrations; *nahash*, a cream cheese and filo pastry, is a Syrian speciality made at this time.

COOKING UTENSILS

Being very old, most of the recipes in this book were originally cooked using unsophisticated utensils on primitive stoves. A modern person cooking the Middle Eastern way needs only three or four basic items in addition to normal kitchen utensils: a large, deep frying pan, preferably made of cast iron; a pestle and mortar; and a blender or food processor.

COOKING INGREDIENTS

Cooking oils are basically vegetable oils such as corn oil and sunflower oil, or various nut oils. Dishes to be eaten cold are made with olive oil, which is the foundation of all dressings.

Samneh is melted butter, clarified by straining the oil through a thin piece of muslin, which extracts any impurities to impart a richer taste. Like *alya*, *samneh* is mainly used by rural communities.

Other items to have in stock for cooking the Middle Eastern way are *bulghur*, or cracked wheat; *tahina* or *tahini*, sesame seed paste; *filo* pastry; flavourings such as orange flower and rose waters; and a supply of almonds, pine nuts, walnuts, and pistachios.

Spice names

The following are Arabic translations of the most commonly used spices – a handy guide for shopping in the souks:

Allspice: *bahar*	Ginger: *zanjibil*
Anise: *anisun*	Mace: *fuljan*
Black pepper: *fil-fil afwad*	Nutmeg: *jawz al-teeb*
Cardamom: *hayl (hababan)*	Paprika: *fil-fil ahmar*
Chilli: *fil-fil ahmar har*	Saffron: *za'fran*
Cloves: *kabsh qaranful*	Sesame seed: *sim-sim*
Coriander: *kusbarah*	Tamarind: *tammar*
Cumin: *kammun*	al-Hindi
Fenugreek: *helba*	Tumeric: *kurkum*

*Making a pitta-bread sandwich in a
Cairo snackbar.*

PAGES 22 AND 23 *A large mezze table
may include up to 70 small dishes.*

Mezze

Even damaged by war, Beirut remains an enchanting city which many other places on the Mediterranean have tried to emulate, but without success. Standing with its feet in the sea and with its back to snow-capped mountains, it is sophisticated and fun-loving. Here you will always eat well, and the nightclubs in Jounieh offer some of the best cabaret in the Middle East.

I first visited Lebanon in 1970 to write some travel articles. In the late seventies I returned to photograph the war-torn city for *The Times*. And in 1993 I went back to find Beirut is on its feet again – life is normal, the shops are busy and restaurants are full.

On my initial visit, a friend and I chose to eat in a restaurant at Pigeon Grotto, which remains a popular family outing on the seafront. Having ordered *mezze*, we were choosing a main course when the *maître d'hôtel* suggested that *mezze* would probably suffice. Imagine our relief, therefore, when plate after plate of starters was brought to the table. Counted, they numbered twenty-five and were obviously a substantial meal.

Essentially a Lebanese creation, *mezze* assume the aura of a banquet when prepared by a cook of repute. A way of life in Lebanon, Syria and Turkey, *mezze* have been adopted by other countries in the Middle East. As many as seventy dishes may be served in a large *mezze* on an auspicious occasion such as a marriage.

Items may be miniatures of a main course or true *hors d'oeuvre*, similar to a Scandinavian *smörgasbord*. Their preparation is time-consuming, but many *mezze* can be made beforehand and chilled. Others such as sautéed testicles should be served fresh for best results. Ideally you need someone to help, either to cook or to take the dishes to the table.

You can plan *mezze* around whatever you like, but there are about a dozen basic items without which even a small *mezze* is incomplete. First, the *mezze* table must always have a basket of freshly baked bread; the round, unleavened bread known vaguely as *khoubz Arabieh*, which is used instead of cutlery to scoop up food. It is also essential for the dips.

Three or four dips are always found on a *mezze* table. The best known is *hummus*, a creamy, pale yellow dip made from mashed chick peas and *tahini* (a paste made from ground sesame seeds), blended with lemon juice and spices. Also popular is *babagannouj*, a pleasant, smoky-tasting dip made from grilled, mashed aubergine, garlic and *tahini*. I love it, one dish of *babagannouj* never being enough as I sit talking, dipping bread in it.

Taramasalata is flesh-coloured purée made from dried and salted grey mullet, or commonly from cod. Bread and celery sticks are dipped into *taramasalata*, which is now so popular you can buy it in the British supermarkets, although the very best is home-made. Made from strained yogurt, thick, creamy *labneh* is always part of a *mezze*. In contrast, a purée of red pepper and walnuts, *muhammara*, is a hot dip. Both keep well in the refrigerator.

Another familiar constituent of *mezze* is stuffed vine leaves. These are popular throughout the Middle East, served either hot, with a minced meat filling, or cold, stuffed with rice and pine nuts.

Lebanese cooking suffers from only one handicap in that there is no good beef available. This is true throughout the Middle East, where nowhere is a cattle country. As mutton is also frequently of poor quality, a great many seasonings are used to compensate for the lack of flavour, and meat is often minced to disguise the tough texture. Usually there are at least two minced meat dishes in a basic *mezze*. *Kibbeh nayé* consists of raw, seasoned minced lamb that is combined with other ingredients, shaped into meatballs, and fried.

Strips of fried liver and *sanbusak* or *börek* (pastries) filled with minced meat, cream cheese and spinach are also popular *mezze*. Artichoke hearts, brains (both with lemon and olive oil dressing), cubes of white cheese, celery, olives and pickled sweet peppers are easy-to-serve cold dishes. And one could go on endlessly listing more dishes – *falafel* (dried and mashed white broad bean patties or croquettes), fried mussels, chicken wings grilled with garlic and yogurt sauce, miniature pizzas . . .

But, finally, there is *tabbouleh*, the Lebanese national salad, without which no *mezze* is complete. Very refreshing, it has a crunchy texture from the cracked wheat and a tangy taste from the lemon. It must be served fresh.

By tradition, *mezze* are eaten with *arak* (*raki* in Turkey), a spirit similar to *pastis* drinks like Pernod.

Kadin Budu "Lady's thighs"

50 g (2 oz) rice

450 g (1 lb) lean minced beef or lamb

2 eggs

1 teaspoon olive oil

1 medium onion, finely chopped

2½ tablespoons very finely chopped parsley

salt and pepper

flour, to coat

100 g (4 oz) butter

SERVES ABOUT 4

First cook the rice as for Plain *pilav* rice (page 78) until just under-done (test a grain with your teeth). Set aside to cool.

Knead the meat well in a large bowl, then add one of the eggs, the cool rice, oil, chopped onion and parsley. Season and mix together very well to form a smooth paste.

With moistened hands, break off lumps of the mixture and shape into walnut-sized balls. Place in a frying pan with a cup of water and simmer gently for 15 minutes. Drain and set aside to cool.

Beat the remaining egg and dip the meat balls in it, then roll them in flour. Fry them in the melted butter over a high heat until they are crisp and brown. Keep warm until ready to serve. Good *kadin budu* should be crispy with a juicy interior.

Babagannouj   Aubergine dip

2 large aubergines
4 tablespoons tahini (sesame
    seed paste)
juice of 1 lemon
2 cloves garlic, crushed
salt and pepper, to taste
1 teaspoon finely chopped
    parsley, to garnish
olive oil, to serve

SERVES ABOUT 4

Slit the skins of the aubergines – this allows the steam to escape during cooking – then bake or grill gently until the outsides are charred and crisp and they begin to split. Cut them in half, scoop out the flesh and mash thoroughly.

Combine with the *tahini*, lemon juice, garlic, salt and pepper and process or blend to a smooth consistency. If the mixture seems too thick, add some water, which will turn it a whiter colour.

Serve in a glass or pottery dish garnished with the chopped parsley and, finally, pour a teaspoon of olive oil into the centre.

Babagannouj is most often eaten as a dip with pitta bread, but it can also be served as a salad with black olives and tomato slices.

Hummus   Chick pea dip

175 g (6 oz) dried chick peas
1 teaspoon salt
1–2 garlic cloves, crushed
salt
150 ml (5 fl oz) tahini (sesame seed paste)
juice of 2–3 lemons
1 tablespoon olive oil
paprika, to sprinkle (optional)
finely chopped parsley, to garnish (optional)

SERVES ABOUT 6

Soak the chick peas in plenty of cold water overnight. Drain, add the salt, cover with water and cook in a pressure-cooker for about 20 minutes, or simmer for 1½ hours in a pan. Drain the chick peas, reserving the liquid, then set aside a few peas for garnish.

Using a little of the cooking liquid, reduce the rest of the chick peas to a purée in a blender or food processor. Add the garlic, salt and *tahini*, and blend together thoroughly. Lastly pour in the lemon juice,

by which time the *hummus* should have a rich, creamy consistency.

Pour into a shallow, concave dish (about the size of a salad plate), pour the oil in the centre and garnish with the whole chick peas. Sprinkle the paprika and a little chopped parsley as a decoration around the edges, if you like.

Hummus should be served at room temperature as a dip with warmed pitta bread. It also makes a tasty accompaniment to grilled kebabs.

Taramasalata   Fish roe dip

4 thick slices stale white bread
4 tablespoons cold milk
100 g (4 oz) fish roe (see method)
1 clove garlic, crushed
½ small onion, finely minced
juice of 1–2 lemons, to taste
1 egg yolk
4 tablespoons olive oil

SERVES ABOUT 4

The most authentic roe to use is *tarama*, the dried and salted roe of the grey mullet. Smoked cod's roe can be used instead, in which case the skins will need to be removed first.

Remove the crusts and soak the bread in the cold milk. Meanwhile pound the roe thoroughly in a mortar or purée in a food processor until it is soft.

Squeeze the bread dry and crumble it into the roe. Add the garlic and onion, half the lemon juice and pound (or blend) to a

creamy paste. When it is smooth, break in the egg yolk and continue to pound or blend while dribbling in the olive oil and the rest of the lemon juice.

Chill and serve as a dip with whole radishes, black olives, celery sticks and pitta bread.

Most *taramasalata* sold commercially is artificially coloured and tastes nothing like this authentic recipe. The home-made version will keep for about 10 days in a sealed container in the refrigerator.

Tahini   Sesame paste dip

2 cloves garlic
salt, to taste
juice of 2 large lemons
6 tablespoons tahini (sesame seed paste)
pinch of ground cumin
1 teaspoon finely chopped parsley

SERVES ABOUT 4

Crush the garlic and salt together. Mix with a little lemon juice and blend with the *tahini*. Add the cumin and remaining lemon juice to form a smooth paste, like peanut butter.

Use more garlic if you want the *tahini* to taste stronger. If it is too thick, reduce it with water. As with *hummus*, a blender is ideal for making *tahini*: the result will be smoother and creamier than if made by hand.

Serve in a bowl, and garnish with the parsley.

A selection of Middle Eastern dips often included as part of a mezze *– Hummus (top), Tahini (centre) and Taramasalata.*

Labneh   Thick yogurt

300 ml (½ pint) natural yogurt
salt, to taste
finely chopped fresh mint, to
garnish
olive oil

SERVES ABOUT 4

Most mezze *tables will offer a selection of dips, including these. Creamy white* labneh *is a wholesome yogurt dip.* Muhammara *(recipe, page 30) is a hot dip excellent with grilled meats. Serve both with pitta bread (page 41).*

Fold a large piece of damp muslin in half, and place over a large bowl. Pour the yogurt into the centre of the cloth, tie the cloth corners together with string and suspend over the bowl overnight.

Remove the yogurt from the cloth, tip into another bowl, stir in salt to taste and chill. Garnish with chopped fresh mint and a trickle of olive oil in the centre.

Labneh will keep for one week in a sealed container in the refrigerator. Serve with pitta bread as a dip. In many Middle Eastern countries it is eaten with olives for breakfast.

Dolma   Stuffed vine leaves

*50 fresh vine leaves, or 350 g
    (12 oz) vine leaves preserved
    in brine, well rinsed*
200 g (7 oz) rice
liberal pinch of salt
1 large onion, finely chopped
2 cloves garlic, crushed
2 teaspoons finely chopped mint
*2 tablespoons finely chopped
    parsley*
pinch of ground allspice
freshly ground black pepper
3 tablespoons olive oil
*450 g (1 lb) finely minced lamb
    or beef*
juice of 1–2 lemons
lemon slices, to garnish
500 ml (16 fl oz) chicken stock
butter

SERVES ABOUT 10

Cut the stems off the vine leaves. If using fresh leaves, blanch single leaves in boiling water for 2–3 minutes, then place in a bowl of cold water to stop the cooking. If using preserved leaves, place them in a large bowl. Cover with boiling water and leave to soak for 10–15 minutes. Place the leaves in cold water and ease the leaves apart. Drain.

Boil the rice in salted water until just tender, then rinse under cold running water and set aside to drain.

Meanwhile, sauté the onion, garlic, herbs and seasonings in the oil. Add the meat and toss until lightly browned. Remove from heat and leave to cool, then add the rice, mixing everything together very well.

To shape, place a drained vine leaf on a work surface, shiny side down, and sprinkle with a drop of lemon juice. Place about 1 tablespoon of the meat mixture near the stem end, then fold in the end and sides and roll up neatly. Repeat this process until all the leaves are stuffed.

Line the base of a large, heavy-based roasting pan with several vine leaves, then arrange the filled rolls in stacks with lemon slices between. Pour in the stock, add dabs of butter to the top and cover with any remaining leaves, or with aluminium foil. Place a heatproof dish on the top to keep the leaves pressed down, cover with a lid and simmer slowly for 1–2 hours, or until the leaves are tender.

Serve the *dolma* lukewarm, sprinkled with lemon juice. Alternatively you may prefer to serve with a garlic, olive oil and lemon juice dressing. Garnish with halved lemon slices.

Muhammara Hot pepper dip

2 medium onions, finely
  chopped
6 tablespoons olive oil
75 g (3 oz) walnut pieces, finely
  chopped
50 g (2 oz) fresh breadcrumbs
  blended with cold water to a
  purée
1 tablespoon paprika (or ½
  teaspoon chilli powder for a
  very hot muhammara), or 1
  small can hot pepper purée
a pinch of ground cumin
salt
1 tablespoon pine nuts sautéed
  in a little oil

SERVES ABOUT 6

Using a deep frying pan, sauté the onions
gently in the oil until soft and golden. Add
the walnuts, the breadcrumb purée, the
paprika (or chilli or hot pepper purée),
the cumin and salt to taste. Continue to
sauté gently on a low heat until the
ingredients are well blended – about 12
minutes.

Remove from the heat, place in a bowl
and garnish with the pine nuts.

Muhammara is eaten as a dip with
bread. It can also be used as a spicy dip
with kebabs, grilled meats and fish. The
Lebanese also eat it as a spread on toast.

Falafel Broad bean patties

450 g (1 lb) dried broad beans
6 spring onions, finely chopped
3 cloves garlic, crushed
6 tablespoons finely chopped
  parsley
1 teaspoon ground cumin
1 teaspoon fresh coriander, very
  finely chopped
salt and cayenne pepper
oil, for deep frying
lemon wedges, to garnish
  (optional)

SERVES ABOUT 6

Soak the beans overnight in plenty of cold
water. The next day, drain, and then skin
them. Grind in a food processor, or pound
in a mortar.

Add all the other ingredients (except for
the oil) and blend or pound to a smooth
paste-like consistency. Leave to stand,
uncovered, for 15 minutes, then chill. The
paste will dry out in the refrigerator and
the *falafel* will be easier to handle.

With moistened hands, take small
lumps, flatten slightly to form a rissole
shape and place on a tray. Prepare the
remaining bean mixture in this manner.

Heat 1 cm (½ inch) oil in a deep frying
pan and fry the rissoles, turning frequently
until they are golden brown. Drain on
paper towels and serve garnished with
lemon wedges, if you like. *Falafel* are
eaten with a side dish of *tahini* dip.

Falafel *are crunchy spiced bean
rissoles. A popular Egyptian
snack, they are usually eaten
dipped in* tahini *(page 26).*

Tabbouleh   Lebanese "national" salad

225 g (8 oz) bulghur (cracked
  wheat)
175 g (6 oz) onion, finely
  chopped
1 tablespoon chopped fresh mint
8 tablespoons chopped parsley
2 medium tomatoes, skinned
  and diced
1 x 5 cm (2 inch) piece
  cucumber, diced
salt and pepper, to taste
3 tablespoons olive oil
3 tablespoons lemon juice
black olives, to garnish

SERVES 6

Soak the *bulghur* in cold water for 1 hour
before preparing the salad. Drain it and
squeeze out the moisture using your
hands. Pat dry on a cloth.

Place it in a bowl with the onion and mix
together well. Add the mint, parsley,
tomato, cucumber, seasonings, oil and
lemon juice, and blend together well.
Above all, *tabbouleh* should have a
distinctive lemony flavour. (I recommend
skinning the tomatoes before you chop
them, but it isn't necessary. It just depends
if you have time or not.)

Serve the salad chilled, in a glass dish,
decorated with a few black olives.

Tabbouleh is eaten scooped up in bread
or, more traditionally, in lettuce leaves.

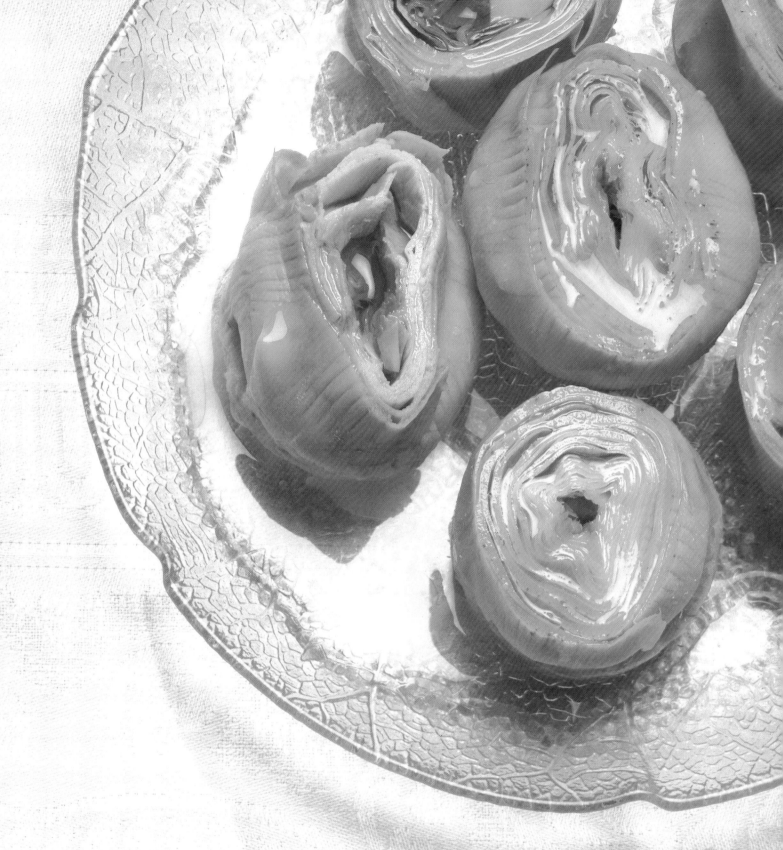

Artichoke Hearts in Olive Oil

6 small fresh artichokes
6 tablespoons lemon juice
2 cloves garlic, halved
6 tablespoons olive oil
salt and pepper

SERVES 4

Remove the stalk and outer leaves of each artichoke and drop the hearts into a bowl of cold water acidulated with a few drops of lemon juice.

Place the hearts in a heavy pan with 400 ml (14 fl oz) water, half the quantities of lemon juice and olive oil and the garlic. Season with salt and pepper, then bring to

the boil. Simmer uncovered until the hearts are tender, 20–30 minutes.

Remove the hearts from the liquid and cool. Mix the rest of the oil and lemon juice with half the remaining liquid, and add more seasoning to taste. Pour over the hearts, cover with cling film and chill until you are ready to eat. Serve cold.

Sanbusak Stuffed crescent pastries

50 g (2 oz) butter
120 ml (4 fl oz) oil
120 ml (4 fl oz) water
1 teaspoon salt
450 g (1 lb) plain flour
egg yolk or milk, to glaze

Sanbusak (or börek in Turkish)
are savoury pastries stuffed with
meat, spinach or cheese. Serve
hot or cold.

MAKES ABOUT 20

To make the pastry, melt the butter gently and pour into a china bowl. Add the oil, water and salt and stir well.

Add the flour, 1 tablespoon at a time, mixing it in thoroughly. Any lumps will gradually disappear. The consistency is correct when pieces of pastry flake off the sides of the bowl, and you can form a ball of smooth pastry in your hands.

While you are stuffing the *sanbusaks* (see right), preheat the oven to 180°C/350°F/Gas 4.

To make a *sanbusak*, break off a ball of pastry, and roll to a circle of about 7.5 cm

(3 inches) in diameter. Put a teaspoon of the filling on one half of the circle, taking care not to over-fill (the mixture expands during the baking), and fold the other half over the filling.

Close the sides of the pastry well by crimping with your fingers and thumb. Continue until all the pastry and filling are used up.

Lay each *sanbusak* side by side on a baking tray, glaze with a little egg yolk or milk, and bake until golden brown, about 30 minutes.

Cheese filling

225 g (8 oz) feta cheese,
  crumbled
pepper
2 hard-boiled eggs, diced
3 tablespoons chopped parsley
  or chives

Mix the ingredients together to form a
paste and stuff the *sanbusak* as described.
It is not necessary to use salt with a salty
white cheese such as feta.

Meat filling

1 medium onion, finely
  chopped
50 g (2 oz) pine nuts, chopped
2 tablespoons butter
225 (8 oz) lean minced lamb
pinch ground allspice
salt and pepper to taste

Sauté the onion and nuts in the butter until
golden. Add the meat, salt, pepper and
allspice, and cook gently until the meat
changes colour, about 10 minutes.
Remove from the pan and cool. Use to stuff
the *sanbusak* as described.

Spinach filling

450 g (1 lb) fresh spinach
1 medium onion, finely
  chopped
olive oil for frying
salt and white pepper
pinch of paprika
100 g (4 oz) feta cheese,
  crumbled

Remove and discard stems and large veins
from the spinach, then wash, drain and
chop the leaves finely.
  Sauté the onion in a little oil until soft
and golden. Add the spinach, seasonings
and mix well and cook until tender.
Allow to cool, then mix in the cheese
before stuffing the *sanbusaks* as
described.

Brains in Lemon and Olive Oil Dressing

4 sets lambs' brains
3 tablespoons vinegar
salt and white pepper, to taste
1/2 onion, sliced
1/2 lemon, sliced
juice of 1 1/2–2 lemons
4 1/2 tablespoons olive oil
1/2 clove garlic, crushed
2 tablespoons finely chopped
   parsley
lemon wedges and extra
   parsley, to garnish

SERVES 4

Soak the brains for 1 hour in water to cover with 2 tablespoons of the vinegar. Rinse under running cold water, then remove all the membranes and grey tissues.

Place the brains in a saucepan with the remaining 1 tablespoon vinegar and warm water to cover. Add salt, onion and lemon slices and simmer gently over a low heat for about 15 minutes.

Remove the pan from the heat and drain the brains, then set aside to cool. Chill for 2–3 hours in a refrigerator.

Slice the brains into quarters. Blend the lemon juice, olive oil, garlic and parsley together and pour over the brains.

Serve chilled with lemon wedges and a garnish of more parsley.

Fried Liver

450 g (1 lb) lambs' or calves' liver
salt and pepper
1 clove garlic, crushed
pinch of paprika
2 tablespoons butter
3 tablespoons lemon juice
parsley, to garnish

SERVES ABOUT 4

Slice the liver into 0.5 cm (1/4 inch) thick strips. Pat dry on kitchen paper.

Rub the salt, pepper and garlic into the liver strips, then sprinkle with paprika.

Melt the butter, add lemon juice and toss the liver in it over a high heat for about 30 seconds each side. Transfer to a dish and serve immediately, garnished with the parsley.

Beid Ghanam   Sautéed lambs' testicles

about 225 g (8 oz) lambs'
   testicles
vinegar
1 clove garlic, crushed
100 g (4 oz) butter
1/2 teaspoon chopped mixed
   herbs
salt and white pepper
juice of 1 lemon
finely chopped parsley, to
   garnish

SERVES ABOUT 4

To clean the testicles, first remove the outer skin by slicing the sac and pushing the testicles out. Separate the sac by cutting the connected duct. Discard the sac and rinse the testicles under cold running water. Soak for 1 hour in water with 2 tablespoons of vinegar. Drain, remove any veins and chop.

Sauté the crushed garlic in melted butter, then add the herbs, salt and pepper. Toss the testicles lightly in the butter until golden brown. Do not overcook. Finally add the lemon juice and serve hot, garnished with chopped parsley.

Some of the more unusual delicacies included in many Middle Eastern mezze: *Brains in lemon and olive oil dressing (top); Fried liver (centre); and* Beid ghanam, *or sautéed lambs' testicles.*

Chicken wings spiked with garlic and lemon juice can be served hot or cold.

Chicken Wings with Garlic and Yogurt

8 chicken wings, cut in half
6 tablespoons lemon juice
2 cloves garlic, crushed
1 teaspoon paprika
salt and white pepper
175 ml (6 fl oz) natural yogurt
cress or parsley, to garnish

SERVES ABOUT 4

Marinate the wings in lemon juice with crushed garlic and seasonings for 1 hour, turning occasionally. Remove and drain.

Mix the yogurt into the marinade, then brush on to the wings. Place under a medium-hot grill. As the yogurt dries, brush more on. The wings should become brown and crisp. Serve warm, garnished with cress or parsley.

Fried Mussels

40 large mussels
oil for deep frying
flour for coating
lemon slices and parsley, to garnish

Batter
15 g (½ oz) dried yeast
120 ml (4 fl oz) tepid water, or enough to make the consistency of single cream
pinch of sugar
salt
75 g (3 oz) plain flour, sifted
1½ tablespoons oil

Tarator sauce
2 slices stale white bread, soaked in water and squeezed dry
65 g (2½ oz) ground almonds or pine nuts
2 cloves garlic, crushed
juice of 1 lemon
6 tablespoons olive oil
salt and pepper, to taste

White sauce
3½ tablespoons butter
salt and pepper
25g (1 oz) flour
about 250 ml (8 fl oz) milk
good pinch of mace

SERVES 6

Make the batter first and allow to stand while preparing the *tarator* sauce, the white sauce and the mussels. Dissolve the yeast in the water with the sugar and salt. When it has frothed, mix into the flour with the oil. The batter should have the consistency of gloss paint.

Mix together all the *tarator* ingredients with a pestle and mortar until they form a creamy paste.

For the white sauce, melt the butter in a small saucepan with salt and pepper. Stir in the flour using a wooden spoon, adding the milk gradually and stirring all the time. Add enough milk so that the sauce becomes sloppy without being thick. Set aside and keep warm.

Wash the mussels under running water, using a brush and knife to remove beards and any barnacles. Discard any that are open. Make sure any sand or grit is thoroughly rinsed off.

Boil the mussels vigorously in salted water until the shells open, about 5 minutes. Discard any that have not opened. Allow the mussels to cool, then remove them from their shells and place on a board. Retain the mussel stock.

Heat the oil in a deep pan. Coat each mussel with white sauce, then dip it in the flour and then the batter. Drop into the sizzling oil, and deep-fry until crisp and golden, about 1 minute on a high heat.

Drain and serve immediately on a plate garnished with fresh parsley and lemon slices with a side dish of *tarator* sauce. Spear the mussels with toothpicks and dip them into the sauce.

In the West, mayonnaise or tartare sauce might be served with these fried mussels.

Mussels fried in batter are common mezze *in Lebanon and Turkey.*

Pickled Chilli Peppers

*450 g (1 lb) long mild chilli
     peppers*
1 small dried chilli
1½ tablespoons salt
300 ml (½ pint) water
*120 ml (4 fl oz) white wine
     vinegar*

Prick the peppers all over so that they
absorb the marinade. Pack together tightly
in a large glass jar with the dried chilli. Add
the salt, water and vinegar, ensuring that
there is no air trapped between the
peppers.

Seal and store for three weeks by which
time the peppers will have softened.
Remove the amount required, drain well
and serve.

Khoubz Arabieh Pitta bread

25 g (1 oz) fresh yeast or
   1 tablespoon dried yeast
pinch of sugar
about 600 ml (1 pint) tepid
   water
½ teaspoon salt
450 g (1 lb) plain flour
oil

MAKES 8

Cool and crisp accompaniments
to pitta bread – salty feta cheese,
black olives and pieces of celery.

Mix the yeast and sugar into a paste with about 4 tablespoons of the water. Set aside until the mixture becomes frothy, 10–15 minutes.

Stir the salt into the flour in a large mixing bowl. Make a well in the centre and stir in the yeast mixture with more of the water. Begin kneading into dough using enough water to reach a firm consistency. The dough must be well kneaded – at least 10 minutes – add a little oil if you find it is too firm at first. When the dough is smooth and elastic, shape into a ball and place in a lightly greased bowl, cover with a damp tea-towel and set aside in a warm place for 1–2 hours, or until the dough has doubled in size.

Lightly flour your work surface. Turn out the dough onto it and punch it down until it is about 0.5 cm (¼ inch) thick. Cut into 8 portions, then roll each portion into a ball and dust with flour. Cover with a dry tea-towel and allow to rise again, about 20 minutes.

Meanwhile, preheat the oven for 15 minutes at 250C°/500F°/Gas 10. Grease a baking sheet and put it in the oven to heat – although be careful the oil does not burn. Using a floured wooden spatula, gently flatten each ball of dough, then lift them on to the heated baking sheet.

Sprinkle water on each leaf to prevent them burning, then bake for about 5 minutes until puffed up. The final result should be a delicate brown leaf with a soft pouch inside. Cool on a wire rack.

Men commonly do the shopping
in many Middle Eastern societies.
Here a Kuwaiti is buying potatoes
on his way to work.

Soups

On one of my frequent visits to Jordan, my driver took the twisting King's Highway *en route* to Petra, via Kerak, a town in the western escarpment. It was late March and from being a sunny day, the weather suddenly turned black, lightning crackled over the Dead Sea and wind drove sheets of hail against our windscreen. Adeb and I had intended stopping only for a coffee in Kerak, a town known for its lofty, Crusader-built castle, but instead we lingered over a warming bowl of soup. Feast-day soup is a traditional dish, especially among Jordan's minority Christian community, of whom many live in this area and around Madaba. Dipping in chunks of bread, we found it sustained us for the rest of our journey.

While soups tend to be uncommon in the hot, desert states, they are widely cooked in countries such as Turkey, Syria and Iraq with colder climates. Old Middle Eastern recipe manuals show an infinite number of meat and vegetable soups and many combinations of both.

Lentil is the most popular, especially in Egypt where *felaheen* may eat it three times a day. The dried pulses that are so widely cultivated in Egypt, Iraq and the Levant – lentils, broad beans, chick peas, split peas and others – make thick, creamy soups or *shorbah* (in Arabic).

Other soups such as vegetable soup are so rich in ingredients that they are almost a stew and, eaten with bread, become a meal in themselves. Common vegetable soups are courgette, carrot and a variety of spinach soups. All use fresh ingredients.

Although I have not given the recipes, two unusual soups from Egypt and Yemen are *melokhia* and *helba*. Made with a game base and fresh *melokhia* leaves (of the mallow family and resembling mint), the first, from ancient Egyptian recipes, is still prepared almost daily by country women, the proportions varying according to their standard of living. *Helba* is a fiery soup, served scalding in earthenware bowls, that is eaten daily throughout Yemen.

Yogurt soups are a major soup category, the addition of yogurt adding a wholesome taste to any food. Often the yogurt is only added at the end, merely stirred in and gently heated. I once enjoyed a splendid yogurt soup in a small hotel in Konya, the town of whirling dervishes in central Anatolia. The Turks also use prodigious amounts of yogurt in their cooking; chilled cucumber and yogurt soup is a perfect start to lunch on a hot summer's day.

Many people will already know *avgolemono* from a Greek restaurant. The same soup, egg and lemon, or *beid bi limoun* in Arabic, is common in Turkey and Lebanon. A very nourishing soup, especially for anyone who is convalescing, the recipe here is only one of many delicate versions.

Fish soups are popular along the coasts of Turkey, Syria and Lebanon. The recipe included here comes from Izmir, the Turkish port known for its annual September trade fair. Coastal restaurants in Lebanon serve wonderful *shorbat al samak* made with fresh Mediterranean fish. Iranians as well as Iraqis enjoy courgette soup, a simple to make first course that never fails to please my guests.

The typical sweet and sour marriage of many sophisticated Persian dishes is found in pomegranate soup, an exotic, if time-consuming, dish to make.

A western touch with many of these soups might be to garnish them with fried croutons.

Tomato Soup

900 g (2 lb) medium tomatoes
1 clove garlic, finely chopped
1 medium onion, finely chopped
pinch of ground coriander
pinch of paprika
salt and pepper, to taste
3½ tablespoons olive oil
600 ml (1 pint) home-made chicken stock
juice of 1 lemon
finely chopped parsley, to garnish

SERVES 6

Scald, peel and seed the tomatoes, then chop them finely. Sauté the garlic, onion, coriander, paprika and seasonings in the olive oil until soft, then add the tomatoes and cook for 5 minutes, stirring.

Add the stock (or use half this quantity of stock made up to 600 ml/1 pint with tinned tomato juice, if desired). Cover and simmer for 15–20 minutes. Allow the soup to cool, then purée in a blender or food processor. Finally stir in the lemon juice, re-heat and serve garnished with parsley.

Carrot Soup

50 g (2 oz) butter
1 level tablespoon ground coriander
450 g (1 lb) carrots, washed, scraped and cut
*   into thin slices*
600 ml (1 pint) chicken stock
pinch of sugar
salt and freshly ground black pepper
75 ml (3 fl oz) single cream
parsley, to garnish

SERVES 4

Melt the butter in a deep frying pan and stir in the coriander. Add carrots and sauté, stirring frequently, until tender, about 15 minutes. Set aside to cool.

Place the carrots in a blender or food processor with the chicken stock, sugar and salt and pepper to taste. Blend until smooth.

When ready to serve, pour the soup into a saucepan, stir in the cream and simmer until hot, but not boiling. Adjust the seasoning and garnish with parsley. This may be eaten hot or chilled.

Chilled Cucumber and Yogurt Soup

1 large cucumber
600 ml (1 pint) natural yogurt
75 g (3 oz) fresh tomato purée
1 clove garlic, finely chopped
salt to taste
pinch of paprika, to garnish

SERVES 4

Wipe the cucumber clean, but do not peel it. Chop coarsely, sprinkle with salt and allow to stand for 30 minutes. Rinse and drain, and put it in a blender with the remaining ingredients (except for the paprika). Blend until the soup is creamy. Chill.

Serve in chilled bowls, each garnished with a sprinkling of paprika.

Yogurt Soup

1 medium onion, finely chopped
50 g (2 oz) butter
450 ml (¾ pint) home-made chicken stock,
*   strained*
50 g (2 oz) pearl barley, soaked overnight
salt and pepper
2 tablespoons finely chopped parsley
1 egg
450 ml (¾ pint) natural yogurt
juice of ½ lemon (optional)
2 tablespoons dried mint, crushed

SERVES 4

Sauté the onion in the butter until soft and golden. Add the chicken stock and simmer until just below boiling point. Add the drained barley and cook until tender – about 20 minutes – then add seasoning and parsley.

Beat the egg lightly, add it to the yogurt and blend together well. Then add a little warm stock to the yogurt and mix. Pour the yogurt slowly into the stock, and stir over a low heat – do not boil or the yogurt will curdle – for 10–15 minutes. A few drops of fresh lemon juice add zest to this delicious soup. Garnish with the mint.

PAGES 46 AND 47
Yogurt is a popular ingredient in Middle Eastern soups, as in these recipes. Chilled cucumber and yogurt soup (top left) is ideal for a summer's day. Easy to make, thick and creamy Carrot soup (top right) is delicious served chilled. The recipe for Yogurt soup has Armenian origins.

Egg and Lemon Soup

*1.2 litres (2 pints) home-made
    chicken stock*
salt and pepper, to taste
50 g (2 oz) rice
2 eggs
juice of 1 medium lemon
parsley, to garnish

SERVES 6

Heat, but do not boil, the chicken stock,
then season with salt and pepper. Add the
rice and simmer until it is tender, 10–15
minutes.

Meanwhile, prepare the sauce. Beat the
eggs in a small bowl, gradually adding the
lemon juice at the same time.

When ready to serve, slowly add the
lemon juice mixture to the soup, which
should be hot but not boiling (the eggs
will curdle if it does boil). Leave to stand
for a few minutes before serving,
garnished with fresh parsley.

Fish Soup

2 medium onions, chopped

2 cloves garlic, crushed

4½ tablespoons olive oil

900 g (2 lb) white fish

1 small crab, cracked

1 handful mussels, beards
   removed and cleaned

1 leek, white part only, chopped

1 tablespoon cider vinegar

1 teaspoon turmeric

½ teaspoon ground allspice

salt and freshly ground black
   pepper, to taste

1 sprig each of fennel and
   savory

2 bay leaves

2 egg yolks

juice of 1 lemon

2 tablespoons finely chopped
   parsley

SERVES 6

Only fresh fish will do for this soup. First sauté the onions and garlic in a little of the olive oil. Transfer this to a deep saucepan and add everything except the egg yolks, lemon juice and parsley. Add 1.25 litres (2¼ pints) water and simmer for 1½ hours until a rich broth is obtained.

Strain this broth to get a clear soup, or simply remove any bones, skin and crab and mussel shells. Some cooks put the fish in a cloth and suspend it over a bowl. The juice is allowed to flow through, and then the cloth wrung out to extract every drop of liquid.

Now beat the egg yolks and slowly add the lemon juice. Take a ladle of the broth and add to this mixture, stirring gently. Finally add the egg and lemon mixture to the saucepan of broth, stir well and simmer on a low heat until ready to serve.

Garnish with the parsley and grind more black pepper over the top.

Feast-day Soup

*salt and freshly ground black
    pepper*
*450 g (1 lb) finely minced lean
    lamb*
*1 medium onion, very finely
    chopped*
pinch of ground cinnamon
50 g (2 oz) rice or vermicelli
*600 ml (1 pint) home-made beef
    stock*
juice of 1 lemon
1 tablespoon butter
chopped parsley, to garnish
*1–2 tablespoons tomato purée
    (optional)*

SERVES ABOUT 4

Season the meat and knead it well. Add the onion and cinnamon and mix thoroughly. With moistened hands, roll the meat into marble-sized balls.

Boil the rice in some water until semi-cooked, then add the stock, meatballs, and lemon juice. Simmer together until the rice is tender, about 15 minutes. Cool.

Reheat just prior to serving, dot with the butter and sprinkle with the parsley. You can add a tablespoon or so of tomato purée to vary this traditional soup from Jordan, if you wish.

Lentil Soup

1 large onion, finely chopped
50 g (2 oz) butter
*200 g (7 oz) lentils, soaked
    overnight and drained*
*1.2 litres (2 pints) home-made
    beef stock*
1 teaspoon ground cumin
*salt and freshly ground black
    pepper*
*3 slices white bread, crusts
    removed, diced*
1 clove garlic, crushed
2 tablespoons olive oil
3 tablespoons lemon juice
*finely chopped parsley, to
    garnish*

SERVES 6

Sauté the onion gently in half the butter until soft, then add the drained lentils and stir until glazed with the butter. Add the stock, cumin and salt and pepper, then simmer until the lentils have almost disintegrated, 1½–2 hours. Test the lentils to make sure they are tender, then cool and purée mixture briefly in a blender or food processor.

Fry the diced bread (or croûtons) in the remaining butter with the crushed garlic.

Return the soup to the pan, reheat, and bring gently to the boil. Leave to stand for a few minutes before serving, then stir in the oil, lemon juice and croûtons. Garnish with a little parsley.

*From Jordan, Feast-day soup
(left) is eaten on auspicious
occasions. Lentil soup (top) enjoys
wide popularity, especially in
Egypt and the Levant – Lebanon,
Syria and Jordan.*

Vegetable and Beef Soup

1 large onion, finely sliced
3 tablespoons olive oil
450 g (1 lb) stewing beef, cubed
1 large potato, peeled and sliced
1 red pepper, seeded and sliced
2 carrots, peeled and thinly sliced
50 g (2 oz) white cabbage, shredded
1.25 litres (2¼ pints) home-made beef stock
1 tablespoon tomato purée
1 teaspoon dill
salt and pepper
2 tablespoons tarragon vinegar
finely chopped parsley, to garnish (optional)

SERVES 6

Using a deep frying pan, sauté the onion gently in the olive oil until it is soft. Add the meat, shaking the pan frequently to prevent the meat from sticking, and cook for 5 minutes. Add the vegetables and cook a further 10 minutes, turning frequently.

Transfer everything to a large, heavy-based saucepan and add the stock, tomato purée, dill and seasoning. Simmer gently on a low heat for 1–1½ hours.

Allow to cool, then remove the fat layer from the top. Reheat just before serving, adding the vinegar as a final touch. Garnish with chopped parsley if you like.

Courgette Soup

3½ tablespoons olive oil

450 g (1 lb) courgettes, washed, dried and thinly
  sliced

2 cloves garlic, crushed

1 large onion, thinly sliced

600 ml (1 pint) home-made chicken stock

3 tablespoons finely chopped parsley

salt and freshly ground white pepper

2 teaspoons lemon juice

SERVES 4

Heat the oil in a large saucepan, then add
the courgettes, garlic and onion, and
simmer for 10–15 minutes on a low heat.
Add the stock, parsley and seasoning and
simmer for 15 minutes.

Allow the soup to cool. Stir in the lemon
juice and then purée the soup in a blender
until almost smooth. Reheat without
boiling and serve immediately.

Picking lettuce in the Jordan valley. Fresh salads are a feature of Middle Eastern meals.

Salads

Some Middle Eastern countries are as much as two-thirds desert – where it may not rain for years – but revenues from oil and gas deposits, and ingenious irrigation techniques, enable even these places to cultivate vegetables.

Drip irrigation, where each plant has its own "dribble tap", means that many of the arid Arabian Gulf states can grow luscious fruits and vegetables. Barren for thousands of years, the desert responds almost magically to water and fertilizers. Sustained on de-salinated water, cucumbers and cabbages grow twice as big as European strains and the regional tomato yield is prodigious.

In the Fertile Crescent, huge dams irrigate thousands of acres of previously arid countryside. In Syria, the Euphrates Dam has opened the dry eastern province of Raqqa to farming. I met Bedouin who had forsaken their nomadic existence to cultivate lettuces and other seedlings outside their tents.

In Jordan, water from the River Yarmuk is diverted through the East Ghor Canal from which feeder canals irrigate farms along the eastern bank of the River Jordan. The area crops two harvests a year, with entire families, even young children, turning out to help.

Crude farm tools in the National Museum in Baghdad attest to the early skills of Mesopotamian farmers. Iraq's largest flood control and irrigation system now centres on the Tharthar Reservoir, which irrigates the arid plains north west of Baghdad. But the greatest dam in the Middle East is the 12,230-foot-long Aswan Dam, in Egypt. The dam has made possible perennial irrigation all along the Nile Valley.

The Arab's fascination with water and his ability to utilize even the smallest amounts, dates back some 3,000 years to when the ancient Egyptians built a vast dam across Wadi Gerrawi. Then, using neither mortar nor mechanization, the Sabaean Tribe in southern Arabia built the giant Marib Dam in what is now known as Yemen. Ancient texts say that the creation of the dam turned the district into a paradise. Strabo writes of abundant fruits and of great flocks of sheep in the meadows. The collapse of the dam inundated hundreds of miles of farmland, and today Marib has been overtaken by seas of drifting sand, with a wall and sluice gate being the only evidence of the dam's existence.

On the barren central plateau of Iran, farmers have for centuries cultivated by means of ingenious subterranean canals, or *kanats*, linking the strings of wells. Similar *falaj* or underground irrigation channels are found in al-Buraimi Oasis on the border of Abu Dhabi and the Sultanate of Oman.

So while some countries are still far from being self-sufficient, it is incorrect only to associate dates with the Arab World. Some of the sweetest, crispest salads I have ever eaten have been in the Middle East.

Salads like *tabbouleh* are often served as a starter. Otherwise, a fresh salad is invariably served with the main course.

As its name implies, *salata Arabieh* belongs to no particular country, but I always associate it with Lebanon. Char-grilled fish and barbecued kebabs always arrive with a bowl of chopped tomatoes, cucumbers and onions, all shiny and inviting beneath a dressing of garlic, lemon juice and olive oil.

Fattouche, a popular Syrian peasant salad, uses crumbled bread as a variation on the theme. Additional flavours can include chopped fresh mint, parsley and coriander.

The recipe for tomato and coriander salad comes from Yemen, where local cooks have devised all kinds of highly original cold sauces and dips. I am equally happy with just a plain tomato and chopped onion salad sprinkled with pepper and drenched in oil and lemon juice. White cheese, local bread and a tomato and onion salad became a favourite lunch when I was staying at the Winter Palace Hotel overlooking the Nile at Luxor in Egypt.

The use of yogurt in salads is common in Middle Eastern cuisines, especially in Turkey and Jordan. Cucumber, nut and yogurt salad is a wonderful summer starter. Another Turkish dish, aubergine salad, is one of my favourites. Cooked spinach also enjoys a close affinity with yogurt, either plain or with garlic. Garlic, of course, is very much prized in the Middle East.

Olive oil, garlic and chopped fresh parsley flavour this Kidney bean salad. The recipe uses dried beans, but you can also use canned kidney beans.

Kidney Bean Salad

400 g (14 oz) dried kidney beans
juice of 1½–2 lemons
4 tablespoons olive oil
salt and black pepper
1 green pepper, chopped
6 spring onions, finely chopped
1 clove garlic, crushed
1 tablespoon chopped parsley, plus extra, to
    garnish

SERVES 4–6

Soak the beans overnight in plenty of cold water, then rinse and drain them. Boil fast for 15 minutes, then simmer for 1½–2 hours until tender, skimming the surface as necessary.

Prepare the dressing by mixing together the lemon juice, olive oil and salt and pepper. Pour over the beans, then mix in the green pepper, onions, garlic and parsley.

Line a bowl with lettuce leaves and tip in the bean salad. Garnish with a little more parsley.

Fattouche

1 medium cucumber
1 stale pitta bread
150 g (5 oz) onion, coarsely chopped
4 spring onions, coarsely chopped (optional)
small lettuce, shredded
4 tablespoons finely chopped parsley
4 medium tomatoes, coarsely chopped
2 tablespoons chopped fresh mint
juice of 2 large lemons
6 tablespoons olive oil
2 cloves garlic, crushed
salt and pepper, to taste

SERVES 4–6

Chop the cucumber, then sprinkle with salt and allow to stand for 30 minutes. Rinse well and pat dry.

Break the bread into small pieces and put in a large mixing bowl. Add the chopped onions, spring onions, lettuce, parsley, tomatoes, mint and cucumber. Mix together well.

Now make a dressing with the lemon juice, olive oil and garlic. Season with salt and black pepper and pour over the salad mixture. Toss together well and chill before serving.

Salata Arabieh

6 medium tomatoes, diced
1 large cucumber, peeled and diced
2 medium onions, finely chopped
2 cloves garlic, finely chopped
1 medium green pepper, seeded and diced
    (optional)
4 tablespoons chopped fresh mint
4 tablespoons finely chopped fresh parsley
juice of 1½–2 lemons
4 tablespoons olive oil
salt and freshly ground black pepper

SERVES 6

Combine all the vegetables in a bowl. Mix the remaining ingredients together and pour over the vegetables. Toss together very well and chill before serving with pitta bread.

PAGES 58 AND 59 *Two traditional Middle Eastern salads that captures the flavours of the region:* Fattouche *(left) and* Salata *Arabieh.*

Cucumber and Raisin Salad with Yogurt

2 medium cucumbers
salt and freshly ground white
*   pepper*
175 ml (6 fl oz) natural yogurt
40 g (1 1/2 oz) raisins
25 g (1 oz) chopped walnuts
2 spring onions, finely chopped
pinch of ground cumin
1 1/2 tablespoons chopped fresh
*   mint*

SERVES 3–4

Slice the cucumbers, sprinkle with salt and leave to drain in a colander for 30 minutes.
    Combine the yogurt, raisins, walnuts, spring onions, cumin and salt and pepper in a bowl. Add the cucumber and mix well. Finally add the mint and chill prior to serving.

Aubergine Salad

3 medium aubergines
salt
6 tablespoons olive oil
3 cloves garlic, crushed
freshly ground black pepper
120 ml (4 fl oz) natural yogurt
pinch each of paprika and
*   cumin*

SERVES 6

Cut the aubergines into 0.5 cm (¼ inch) thick slices. Sprinkle with salt and leave for 30 minutes, weighted down with a flat dish to help remove the bitter juices. Rinse the aubergine slices and pat dry on kitchen paper.
    Sauté the slices in very hot oil until they are crisp on both sides. Drain on kitchen paper.
    Mix the garlic and salt and pepper into the yogurt. Arrange the aubergine slices in layers in a flat serving dish and coat well with the yogurt. Sprinkle with the paprika and cumin, chill and serve.

Spinach Salad

450 g (1 lb) fresh spinach
175 ml (6 fl oz) natural yogurt
1 clove garlic, crushed
pinch of cumin
salt and pepper

SERVES 4

Clean the fresh spinach under running water and remove the stems and any large veins. Chop the leaves and simmer in their own juices until tender, about 20 minutes. Cool.
    Blend the yogurt with the garlic, cumin and seasonings. Add to the spinach and mix well. Chill until ready to serve.

Salads are especially popular in Turkey and Iran. This selection includes Cucumber and raisin salad with yogurt (top left), Aubergine salad (top right) and Spinach salad. Each salad is delicious served with pitta bread.

Tomato and Coriander Salad

6 firm, ripe medium tomatoes
½ bunch fresh coriander leaves,
  chopped
pinch of paprika
salt and freshly ground black
  pepper
2½ tablespoons olive oil
juice of 1 lemon

SERVES 4

Scald, peel and slice the tomatoes into a bowl. Sprinkle with the chopped coriander leaves.

Combine the paprika, salt and pepper, oil and lemon juice, and beat vigorously. Pour over the tomatoes, then chill. Remove from the refrigerator 10 minutes before serving.

Salata Fil-Fil   Green pepper salad

4 medium green peppers
juice of 1½–2 lemons
4 tablespoons olive oil
dash of vinegar
1 clove garlic, crushed
salt, to taste
black olives, to garnish

SERVES 4

Slice or quarter the green peppers lengthwise, and remove the seeds. Char under the grill until the edges are brown and crisp. Allow to cool.

Make the dressing by mixing together the remaining ingredients, then pour over the peppers. Mix well, and garnish with one or two black olives.

Potato Salad

900 g (2 lb) new potatoes,
  scrubbed
good pinch of cumin
4 tablespoons olive oil
juice of 1½–2 lemons
3 cloves garlic, crushed
salt and pepper
3 tablespoons finely chopped
  spring onions
4 tablespoons finely chopped
  parsley

SERVES 4–6

Boil the potatoes until they are just tender. Allow to cool a little, then cut into uniform chunks. Sprinkle with cumin.

Prepare the dressing by mixing together the oil, lemon juice, garlic and salt and pepper. Pour over the potatoes. Toss well, then chill until required and serve sprinkled with the spring onions and parsley.

The variety of produce in these salads reflects the many vegetables featured in Middle Eastern cooking. Try Salata Fil-Fil (top left), Potato salad (centre) and Tomato and coriander salad.

French Bean, Leek and Asparagus Salad

450 g (1 lb) prepared vegetables
(see method)
salt and freshly ground black
pepper
1 clove garlic, crushed
4½ tablespoons olive oil
juice of 1½–2 lemons

SERVES 4

This salad can be made with any variety of green beans, leeks or asparagus. Top, tail and slice the beans if large; wash and slice the leeks; scrape and trim the asparagus stalks.

Cook each vegetable in a little salted water until barely tender, then drain and allow to cool.

Make a dressing by mixing together the garlic, oil and lemon juice with salt and pepper. Pour over the salad just before serving.

A merchant and his carrot mountain in the Nile delta. Carrots are just one of the colourful vegetables sold in Middle Eastern markets.

Vegetables and Rice

While the western vogue for vegetarian cooking has only recently elevated vegetables to "main course" status, vegetables have a historically important position in a Middle Eastern menu. A frequently quoted saying during Abbasid times was: "A table without vegetables is like an old man devoid of wisdom."

Many dishes such as vegetable casserole are meals in themselves. So is stuffed aubergine, a great favourite of Abbasid society, the Caliph Wathiq being reportedly so fond of aubergines that he ate forty at a time. Iraqis transform the humble potato with a minced meat and pine nut filling, while the stuffed tomatoes of Egypt and the Levant have no equal.

While many Middle Eastern cities today have large, western-style supermarkets, people still turn to the traditional souks for buying fresh vegetables. Store owners display an artistic bent with colourful arrangements of polished tomatoes, shiny courgettes, red and green peppers and purple aubergines. It is unthinkable not to be able to select your own vegetables, which are hunted down as soon as the souk opens. Usually the cook or a servant does the shopping, but in some countries it might be the grandmother with one of the servant's sons to carry her basket.

I especially remember an old Palestinian lady, possibly blind, groping slowly through the vegetable market in East Jerusalem. No doubt she knew her way and was probably a familiar figure, small, wrinkled and wearing a long, black robe. Stopping outside one shop, she felt around the display, then held up a smooth skinned aubergine, handing her purse trustingly to the owner for him to extract payment. While waiting, she popped a grape into her mouth; then smiling like a guilty child, she continued her shopping. I watched her buying a lettuce, lemons and bundles of coriander before losing sight of her in the crowds.

In conservative Arab states such as Qatar and Kuwait, it is common for men to do the shopping. By contrast, in Sana'a, well-veiled women sell onions, carrots, tomatoes and other vegetables coaxed from the rocky soil.

The most commonly used Middle Eastern vegetables – courgettes, peppers, spinach and so on – are available in Britain. If you have trouble finding others, such as okra, try an Indian shop. Always bring home parsley to garnish dishes, and when cooking the Middle Eastern way, never be without a lemon.

Several recipes in this chapter are ideal for vegetarians: the popular *Imam bayıldı* (or swooning Imam), cabbage rolls, okra in oil and bean stew could make an entire buffet. Iran's contribution is an unusual combination of herbs and nuts in an omelette. Spinach is supposed to be native to Iran, but the recipe for spinach pie comes from Turkey, a delicious party dish which can be eaten hot or cold.

Wheat and rice are the main grains used in Middle Eastern cooking. Cracked wheat, or *bulghur*, is more usually encountered in minced meat dishes, but it can be eaten plain with butter, topped with a fresh tomato purée or garlic-flavoured yogurt with black pepper.

Rice is the basic dish throughout the Middle East: *roz* to the Arabs, *pilav* (cooked with other ingredients) in Turkey and *chelo* (steamed) or *polo* (cooked with other ingredients) in Iran. Basmati rice, which resembles the high-grade southern rice, is preferred, often coloured with saffron or turmeric. A common way of serving it is in a ring garnished with a sauce and nuts. Meats and fish are frequently served on a bed of rice, a good example being the Bedouin whole roast lamb. Following a visit to Iran in 1971, I encountered *chelo*, a rice so subtle that I tend to make it to this day, the exception being saffron rice to serve with fish.

Last, but vital to millions of poorer people in the Middle East, are the dishes based on dried beans and peas: the bean dish, *foul medames*, is almost the national dish of Egypt. Most bean and lentil recipes are geared to peasant tastes – chick peas have already appeared in this book in the guise of *hummus*, and there is a recipe for lentil soup, along with lamb and chick pea casserole in the meat chapter.

We know that Middle Eastern cooks use a great deal of yogurt. Natural, or spiked with garlic, it can be served with fried, sautéed or baked vegetables. Lemon juice is routinely used to heighten the flavour of many vegetable dishes such as cabbage rolls or baked aubergine.

Batata Charp Stuffed potatoes

8 medium potatoes
1 egg
1 tablespoon cornflour
salt and pepper
120 ml (4 fl oz) vegetable oil

Filling
1 medium onion, finely
*   chopped*
40 g (1½ oz) butter
pinch each of paprika, ground
*   coriander and allspice*
225 g (8 oz) lean minced beef

SERVES 4–6

First make the filling. Sauté the onion in the butter until golden and soft. Add the seasonings, then the meat. Cook for about 5 minutes until it changes colour. Remove and set aside.

Peel and boil the potatoes. Mash well in a large bowl, then add the egg, cornflour and salt and pepper. Mix in very thoroughly. With moist hands break off a lump the size of a golf ball. Roll it in your hands, then flatten on your work surface and make a small hollow in the top. Fill this with a teaspoonful of the meat mixture and close the edges. Roll the potato ball around in your hands to ensure the meat is well sealed inside. Repeat this procedure until all the meat and potato are used up. Refrigerate the potato balls for at least 1 hour.

Heat the oil in a deep saucepan. When the oil is sizzling, gently lower a potato ball into the saucepan and cook quickly, turning on all sides until it is golden brown. Cook each ball separately and be careful it does not break. Drain well on kitchen paper.

This amount makes about 15 potato balls. Serve with a chopped salad, bread and a *labneh* (page 28) dip.

Stuffed Tomatoes

4 large firm tomatoes
salt and pepper
1 onion, finely chopped
5 tablespoons olive oil
75 g (3 oz) rice
pinch sugar
1 tablespoon currants
1 tablespoon pine nuts, chopped
1 tablespoon finely chopped
*   mint*
1 tablespoon finely chopped
*   parsley*

SERVES 4

Select tomatoes of a uniform size. Carefully slice off the tops and set aside. Scoop out the pulp with a small spoon, removing any hard core, then chop the pulp. Sprinkle the inside of each tomato case with salt and pepper, and leave upside down to drain.

Sauté the onion gently in the olive oil until soft and golden. Add the tomato pulp, and the remaining ingredients, and simmer on a low heat for 3 minutes. Add 150 ml (¼ pint) water and cook gently until the rice softens, about 10 minutes. Meanwhile preheat the oven to 180°C/ 350°F/Gas 4.

Allow the mixture to cool, then spoon it into each tomato case, leaving enough room for the rice to swell. Top each tomato with its own "lid", and arrange side by side in an oiled baking dish. Brush each with a little extra oil and bake for 30 minutes.

Imam Bayildi   Baked aubergine

3 medium aubergines
salt
175 g (6 oz) chopped onion
6 tablespoons olive oil
3 cloves garlic, crushed
1 small red pepper, seeded and diced
3 medium tomatoes, skinned and finely chopped
2 tablespoons pine nuts, chopped
1½ tablespoons raisins, chopped
½ teaspoon paprika
juice of 1 lemon
extra olive oil, to finish

SERVES 6

Cut the aubergines in half lengthways. Using a spoon, scoop out the flesh, being careful not to puncture the skins. Leave a case about 0.5 cm (¼ inch) thick. Chop and salt the pulp, place in a colander, and leave to drain for 1 hour. Rinse under cold running water then pat dry with kitchen paper. Rinse and dry the cases as well.

Fry the onion in some of the oil until it softens. Mix in the garlic and cook for a further 3 minutes. Stir in the aubergine pulp, the pepper and tomatoes, and cook over a medium heat until the pepper softens and most of the liquid has evaporated. Remove the pan from the heat and mix in the pine nuts, raisins, paprika and salt.

Preheat the oven to 180°C/350°F/Gas 4, and put the remaining oil in an ovenproof dish. Arrange the aubergine cases in it, in a close-fitting layer. Fill each case with the stuffing and sprinkle with lemon juice.

Gently add boiling water down one side of the baking dish to come about half-way up the aubergines. Cover with foil and bake in the oven for about 1 hour. Remove the dish when the cases are tender, and allow the aubergines to cool in the sauce.

When the aubergines are cold, drain off excess liquid and trickle a little extra olive oil over the cases. Chill until about 10 minutes before serving.

Stuffed vegetables are always popular with Middle Eastern cooks. Stuffed potatoes (top left) are a favourite in Iraq. Stuffed tomatoes (top right) are delicious eaten either hot or cold. Stuffed aubergines, here ready for the oven, is a medieval Turkish dish that has never fallen out of favour.

Baked Aubergine with Cumin

900 g (2 lb) medium aubergines
6 cloves garlic, crushed
4 tablespoons olive oil
1 teaspoon paprika
1 heaped teaspoon ground
  cumin
2 pinches cayenne pepper
salt
butter
lemon juice

SERVES 4

Preheat the oven to 220–230°C/425–450°F/ Gas 7–8.

Wash and dry the aubergines. Slit the skin in several places to prevent them bursting, then steam until tender, 30–40 minutes (in a pressure cooker, 12–15 minutes). Allow to cool, then cut each aubergine into three strips lengthways. Sprinkle with the garlic.

Heat the oil in an ovenproof dish in the oven. Put the aubergines in and sprinkle

with paprika, cumin, cayenne pepper, salt and dabs of butter. Bake for 5 minutes.

Just before serving, sprinkle with a few drops of fresh lemon juice.

Cabbage Rolls

100 g (4 oz) rice

3 tablespoons olive oil

2 medium onions, finely chopped

2 cloves garlic, crushed

2 tablespoons pine nuts, chopped

pinch each of ground cumin, ground allspice and paprika

225 g (8 oz) finely minced lamb

1 tablespoon dried mint

salt

12 large cabbage leaves

lemon juice (optional)

2 medium tomatoes, skinned and chopped (optional)

cream (optional)

SERVES 6

Cook the rice as for Plain *pilav* rice (page 78).

To make the stuffing, heat the oil in a large frying pan and sauté the onions, garlic and pine nuts with the spices until golden. Add the lamb and mint with a pinch of salt and cook lightly, turning frequently in the pan. Meanwhile, preheat the oven to 180°C/350°F/Gas 4.

Make sure you use large, whole cabbage leaves. Plunge the leaves into boiling salted water to make them pliable, then spread them out on a wooden board and cut out the cores. Place a portion of stuffing on each leaf and roll up into a neat packet, fold up the end and fold in the sides.

Arrange the rolls close together in a shallow, greased ovenproof dish and add slightly salted water to almost cover. Make sure they are tightly packed or they might unwrap.

Cover and cook for 30 minutes, or until the leaves are tender. Serve hot sprinkled with lemon juice, or a sauce made from tomatoes and cream puréed together, as preferred.

French Bean Stew

900 g (2 lb) French beans

Tomato sauce
3 cloves garlic, crushed
½ teaspoon ground coriander
2 tablespoons olive oil
2 medium onions, chopped
1½ tablespoons tomato purée
6 medium tomatoes, skinned
1 tablespoon chopped parsley
salt and white pepper
½ teaspoon paprika
juice of 1 lemon

SERVES 6

First, prepare the tomato sauce. Sauté the garlic and coriander in the oil, then add the onions and cook the mixture for 10 minutes, stirring occasionally. Add the tomato purée, tomatoes and parsley and crush and blend into a purée. Mix in the salt, pepper, paprika and lemon juice and simmer uncovered for 15 minutes. Stir frequently to make a rich, aromatic sauce.

Trim the beans as necessary and place in a large saucepan with the sauce and enough water to barely cover. Simmer until tender, about 15 minutes.

If you prefer your beans *al dente*, remove after 10 minutes and set aside while you reduce the sauce to a thicker consistency. Return the beans to the sauce and re-heat to serve.

Courgettes with Tomatoes

900 g (2 lb) courgettes
2 cloves garlic, crushed
pinch of ground coriander
3 tablespoons olive oil
6 medium tomatoes, skinned
    and chopped
salt and black pepper
1½ tablespoons chopped
    parsley
120 ml (4 fl oz) lemon juice

SERVES 4

Wash and dry the courgettes, and slice into moderately thick rounds.

Sauté the garlic and coriander in the oil, then add the courgette slices. Cook gently for about 15 minutes, turning frequently.

Add the tomatoes, salt and pepper, parsley, lemon juice and 120 ml (4 fl oz) water. Simmer until tender, about 20 minutes. Serve hot.

Okra Stew

6 medium tomatoes, sliced
450 g (1 lb) fresh okra
cider vinegar
3 cloves garlic, crushed
2 medium onions, finely
  chopped
1 teaspoon coriander

3 tablespoons olive oil
salt and pepper
1 tablespoon tomato purée
ground cumin
juice of 1 lemon

SERVES 4

Scald, skin and slice the tomatoes. Wash and cut off the okra stems, taking care not to puncture the pods. Soak the okra for 30 minutes in vinegar to prevent them becoming sticky during cooking. Drain and rinse under running water.

Sauté the garlic, onions and coriander in the olive oil until soft. Add the okra and cook gently for 5–10 minutes, stirring occasionally.

Place half the okra mixture in a greased flameproof casserole and cover with a layer of sliced tomato. Make another layer of onion and okra and arrange more tomatoes on top. Season with salt and pepper and top with the remaining tomatoes.

Mix tomato purée with a little water and pour over the vegetables, then add enough water to almost cover the top layer of tomatoes. Add a good pinch of cumin. Simmer over a medium heat about 10 minutes. Meanwhile, preheat the oven to 180°C/350°F/Gas 4.

Remove from the heat, add lemon juice and bake in oven until the okra are quite tender, 30–40 minutes. Serve hot in the casserole.

Slow, gentle cooking brings out the flavours of these vegetable dishes: French bean stew (below left); Okra stew (top right) and Courgettes with tomatoes.

Herb and Nut Omelette

3 tablespoons butter

6 spring onions, finely chopped

2 lettuce leaves, finely chopped

1 teaspoon dried dill, or 2½ tablespoons fresh dill

4 tablespoons chopped parsley

8 eggs

saffron to colour, or ¼ teaspoon turmeric

a pinch of cinnamon

salt and pepper

a pinch of bicarbonate of soda

25 g (1 oz) chopped walnuts

25 g (1 oz) raisins, roughly chopped (optional)

SERVES 4

Melt half the butter in a frying pan with an ovenproof handle. Add the spring onions, lettuce, dill and parsley and sauté until the spring onions are transparent. Add the remaining butter and allow to melt.

Preheat the oven to 180°C/350°F/Gas 4.

Beat the eggs well, then add saffron (or turmeric), cinnamon, salt and pepper and bicarbonate of soda. Stir in the nuts, and the raisins, if you are using them. Pour this mixture into the frying pan but do not stir. Transfer to the preheated oven and bake until golden and set.

Serve immediately, either alone or with a tomato salad.

Baked Squash in Tahini Sauce

4 medium yellow squash

100 g (4 oz) butter

3 medium onions, finely
  chopped

4 cloves garlic, crushed

pepper

½ teaspoon ground coriander

½ teaspoon paprika

¼ teaspoon ground cinnamon

450 g (1 lb) lean minced lamb
  or beef

salt

4 tablespoons tahini (sesame
  seed paste)

5 tablespoons lemon juice, or
  more

SERVES 4–6

Preheat the oven to 190°C/375°F/Gas 5.
Peel the squash and slice into rounds
about 1 cm (½ inch) thick. Sauté in the
butter until almost cooked and golden. Set
aside.

In the same pan, sauté the onions and
half of the crushed garlic. Season with
pepper, coriander, paprika and cinnamon,
then add the meat and cook until lightly
brown. Add salt.

Line a greased ovenproof dish with a
layer of closely packed squash, spread the
meat mixture over it, then layer with
remaining squash.

Blend together the *tahini*, lemon juice,
remaining garlic and salt to taste in a bowl.
Blend to the consistency of paste, adding

more lemon juice if necessary. Pour
this into the casserole and bake until the
top turns a golden brown, about 40
minutes.

Turkish Vegetable Casserole

1 medium aubergine, sliced
salt

4 medium okra, each about
  7.5 cm (3 inches) long

2 medium onions, chopped

5–7 tablespoons olive oil

1 green pepper, seeded and
  chopped

4 medium courgettes, unpeeled
  and coarsely chopped

100 g (4 oz) beans, chopped

100 g (4 oz) green peas

450 g (1 lb) potatoes, peeled and
  cubed

4 cloves garlic, crushed

1 bunch of parsley, finely
  chopped

2 teaspoons paprika

1 heaped teaspoon ground
  cumin

350 ml (12 fl oz) chicken or
  vegetable stock

5–6 medium tomatoes, peeled
  and sliced

1 teaspoon sugar

SERVES 6–8

Soak the aubergine slices in salted water for 30 minutes, then remove and drain well. Prepare okra as for Okra stew (page 73). Preheat the oven to 190°C/375°F/Gas 5. Sauté the onions in a little of the oil until soft and golden. Transfer to a casserole and add the remaining vegetables, except the tomatoes. Add the garlic, parsley, all the seasonings, stock and most of the olive oil. Mix together, then add the tomatoes and dribble in the remaining olive oil. Finally flatten the vegetables down with a wooden spoon.

Cover and bake for about 1 hour or until the vegetables are tender. Remove the casserole, add salt to taste and the sugar, stir well and cook a further 15–20 minutes.

Serve the vegetable casserole with bread as a hot dip. The Turks calls this *turlu guvec* and they like to serve it cold.

Spinach Pie

450 g (1 lb) filo pastry, thawed if frozen

300 ml (½ pint) olive oil

Filling

1.25 kg (2½ lb) fresh spinach (or thawed frozen spinach)

salt and pepper

2 medium onions, chopped

1½ tablespoons butter

4 large eggs, beaten

225 ml (8 fl oz) milk, warmed

225 g (8 oz) feta cheese, crumbled (or Parmesan and feta cheeses mixed)

2 teaspoon dried dill

1 heaped teaspoon paprika

SERVES 6–8

First prepare the filling. If using fresh spinach, wash it, remove the stalks and any large veins, and cut the leaves into thin strips. Sprinkle with salt and leave for 1 hour. Then rub the leaves and squeeze out all the liquid. Follow package instructions for frozen spinach.

Sauté the onions in the butter until transparent. Beat the eggs in a bowl. Blend in the warm milk and add the onions, cheese, dill and paprika. Mix well with the spinach. Add salt and pepper to taste.

Preheat the oven to 180°C/350°F/Gas 4. Grease a 25 x 30 cm (10 x 12 inch) overproof dish.

Brush one side of one sheet of the pastry with oil and lay it in the dish which it will overlap. Brush five more sheets individually with oil and place them on top. Now place the spinach filling on this and trickle 2 tablespoons olive oil over it.

Bring the overlapping pastry up over the filling. Cut the last six sheets to the size of the dish, brush them individually with oil and lay them on top.

Score the top into squares and sprinkle with water to prevent the edges curling. Bake until the top is golden brown, about 30–45 minutes. Allow to set before cutting.

Saffron Rice

400 g (14 oz) long-grain rice
salt
3 tablespoons pine nuts
2 medium onions, finely
  chopped
2 tablespoons olive oil
2 tablespoons raisins
saffron to colour, or ½
  teaspoon tumeric

SERVES 4

Boil rice in salted water briskly for 2–3 minutes in a saucepan. Remove from heat and rinse in a sieve until the water is clear. Set aside to drain.

Sauté the pine nuts and onions in the oil. Add the raisins and the rice, stirring gently for 1–2 minutes until the rice grains are well coated. Return the rice mixture to a saucepan, add the saffron or tumeric, a pinch of salt and water to come 2.5 cm (1 inch) above the surface. Stir, then simmer gently uncovered until all the water is absorbed. Set aside 10 minutes before stirring and serving:

Chelo Persian steamed rice

400 g (14 oz) long-grain rice
salt
50 g (2 oz) butter, melted
4 egg yolks (optional)

SERVES 4

Put the rice and salt in a saucepan and boil briskly for 12–13 minutes. The rice should be soft, but not quite done. Rinse under cold running water until the water is clear, then set aside to drain.

Pour half the melted butter mixed with a little water into a saucepan with a thick base. Add the rice, smoothing it out.

Fold a clean tea-towel in half and place it over the top of the saucepan, then cover with a lid. The tea-towel will absorb the steam, helping the rice to remain fluffy with each grain separate. The bottom should be crisp – ensure it does not burn from being on a too high heat. Cook for about 15 minutes.

Trickle the remaining butter over the rice and serve. The Persian way to serve this is to pop an egg yolk in a hollow made in each portion of the *chelo*.

Plain Pilav Rice

400 g (14 oz) long-grain rice
salt
2 tablespoons olive oil

SERVES 4

Put rice and salt in a saucepan of water and boil briskly for 2–3 minutes. Remove from heat and rinse in a sieve under cold running water until the water is clear. Set aside to drain.

Return the rice to a saucepan, add a small pinch of salt and the olive oil. Cover with cold water to 2.5 cm (1 inch) above the level and stir. Simmer uncovered until all the water is absorbed and small steam holes appear on the surface of the rice, about 15 minutes. Do not stir during the cooking time. Set aside for 5–10 minutes.

Rice is a staple ingredient served throughout the Middle East, and these recipes reflect the varied ways it is prepared. Plain pilav rice (top); Chelo, or Persian steamed rice (centre) and Saffron rice, delicious for serving with seafood.

The peoples of the Gulf State are big seafood-eaters, taking advantage of the abundant selection of fish in coastal waters. Here is a fisherman with part of his day's catch in Dhofar, along the Arabian Sea coast of Oman.

Seafood

Some of my most memorable meals in the Middle East have been seafood – but then I love fish. The setting of many seafood restaurants is also a bonus. How could I forget grilled fish by the creaking water wheels on the Orontes river at Hama, in Syria?

There is a restaurant near the Roman city of Jerash, in Jordan, which serves wonderful grilled perch – known locally as St Peter's fish – from the Sea of Galilee. More rustic is a restaurant in Aqaba with *al fresco* tables under half a dozen straggly palms. The fish is good – you choose your own in the kitchen – but the smell of the charcoal grill attracts Aqaba's 100,000 cats who practically drag it off your table.

Baghdad is famous for open-air restaurants serving *mashgouf* or smoked fish along the banks of the Tigris. The Iraqis do interesting things with fish, especially in the delta port of Basra, but some of the best seafood dishes are found in the Arabian Gulf. Despite oil spillages, the tepid waters of the Gulf abound in seafood: fish, crab, giant prawns and a delicately flavoured, flat-chested cousin of the lobster known as *Umm Robien*.

The early-morning fish markets of Manama, capital of Bahrain, Kuwait, Dubai and the other Gulf states are a hive of activity the moment the *dhows* unload. In Omani towns on the Arabian Sea, sardines and other small fish are sold straight out of the small fishing boats or *houris*.

The Red Sea off Yemen and Saudi Arabia is equally rich in fish: barracuda, bass, cod, lobster and crabs. While the *Quran* imposes no dietary restrictions, shellfish are avoided by many Muslims, a parallel with Judaic dietary laws which forbid eating any fish without fins or scales.

And while the Mediterranean lapping southern Europe grows daily more toxic, the Eastern Mediterranean and the Aegean supply Turkey, Syria and Lebanon with a veritable treasure trove of seafood. One of the many delights of Istanbul is lunch at a sunny seafood restaurant beneath the Galatea Bridge linking the European and Asian sides of the city. At night seafood restaurants along the Bosphorus are packed.

The world's finest caviar comes from the Caspian Sea in northern Iran. The sturgeon are netted as they congregate to spawn and the eggs are scooped from the living fish. During travels around the Caspian Sea, I ate beluga caviar daily for lunch, with a raw onion, lemon, salty butter and local bread. Then back in Tehran, I enjoyed beluga caviar with sour cream and *blinis*.

The most popular fish in the Middle East are red mullet (known by the grand title of *Sultan Ibrahim* in Arabic), *arous*, a fish like the French *daurade* or sea bream, sole, sea bass, tuna and turbot.

Among freshwater fish, the *chaboute* (similar to a trout) is netted in the Tigris-Euphrates river systems in Iraq. This is the famous *mashgouf* which is cleaned, split, staked and smoked around an open fire. Pungent and tender, it is impossible to copy in a kitchen. In Basra, fish baked in date purée is popular.

Tuna and swordfish *kebabs* are a speciality of Turkey where coastal restaurants also serve stuffed mussels and squid. *Samak mashi* or stuffed fish, fish baked in *tahini* sauce and baked fish eaten with *muhammara* are common in Syria and Lebanon. Arabs eat basically the same fish dishes, although an Indian influence has made seafood curries equally popular. Nile fish tend to taste muddy, but there are good seafood restaurants in Suez and Alexandria, *saadiyeh*, or plain fish and rice, and grilled or fried small fish being common dishes.

Some Middle Eastern countries still enjoy traditional dried, salted fish. A common sight in Dhofar, in southern Oman, are sheets of silver sardines drying along the beaches.

Wasif, tiny fish like sprats, are salted and dried by fishermen on the Tihama coast of Yemen. Trucked to the mountain towns, they are sold by the basketful in local souks. The fish adds zest to *zahawiq*, a popular Yemeni dip made from tomatoes and chillies.

Essentials for cooking fish the Middle Eastern way are plenty of olive oil, lemon juice and cumin. Vine leaves, or silver foil as a substitute, are also used for grilling and baking. Skewers are needed for fish kebabs, and a fish clamp will prevent large, whole fish from breaking when you turn them in the oven.

Cold Fish in Olive Oil

*1 × 900 g (2 lb) whole fish (cod,
  bass, mackerel or similar),
  gutted*

6 tablespoons olive oil

*1 large green pepper, seeded
  and finely chopped*

2 medium onions, sliced

3 cloves garlic, crushed

*6 medium tomatoes, peeled and
  sliced, or a 400 g (14 oz) can*

1 tablespoon tomato purée

*a bunch of parsley, finely
  chopped*

salt and pepper

*6 green and 6 black olives, to
  garnish*

SERVES 4

Wash the fish and scrape off any loose
scales if necessary and pat dry on a kitchen
paper. If the skin is thick, make several
diagonal slits to aid cooking. Heat the oil
in a large pan and fry the fish slowly,
cooking lightly on both sides (about 10
minutes). Lift it out gently, drain on
kitchen paper and allow to cool.

Sauté the green pepper in the same oil,
then add the onions after 10 minutes and
cook until both are soft. Add the garlic and
sauté for a further 2 minutes. Pulp the
tomatoes and blend with the purée and
parsley. Add to the pan, season to taste, stir
well and simmer for 15 minutes.

Lift the fish carefully back into the pan,
cover with the sauce and cook gently for
10–15 minutes or until tender. If the sauce
is too thick, add a little water mixed with
lemon juice.

Finally, remove the fish to a large
serving dish and pour the sauce over it.
Surround it with the olives, cool and then
refrigerate. Remove about 10 minutes
before eating.

Prawn Curry

8–10 Dublin Bay prawns
2 tablespoons olive oil
juice of 1 large lemon
salt and black pepper
3 medium onions, sliced
1 bay leaf
1 celery stalk
2 cloves garlic, crushed
1½ tablespoons clarified butter
2.5 cm (1 inch) fresh root ginger,
    peeled and grated
1 level teaspoon turmeric
1 teaspoon ground coriander
½ teaspoon ground cumin
½ teaspoon chilli powder
1 heaped tablespoon desiccated
    coconut
4 medium tomatoes, skinned
    and chopped
freshly chopped coriander

SERVES 4

First prepare the prawns: remove the shells and heads and marinate in olive oil and some of the lemon juice with seasoning for 2 hours.

Put the shells in a pan, cover with cold water, add 3 slices onion, a bay leaf, celery stalk and salt and pepper. Simmer until you have a rich, aromatic stock. Strain well and set aside.

In a large saucepan, sauté the garlic and remaining onion in the clarified butter until soft and transparent. Add the spices and coconut and sizzle for 1 minute.

Now add the tomatoes and remaining lemon juice and cook for 10 minutes, stirring well. Stir in the stock, marinade and prawns, and simmer uncovered until the prawns are tender and the sauce is reduced, 15–20 minutes.

Garnish with finely chopped coriander leaves and serve with *pilav* rice (page 78).

This recipe is based on a popular dish made from Umm Robien, *a type of lobster found in the Arabian Gulf. It can be adapted to shrimp, crayfish or other shellfish.*

Fried Fish

*12 small fish, such as fresh
sardines or herrings*
2 cloves garlic, finely chopped
¹/₂ teaspoon ground cumin
salt and white pepper
*1¹/₂ tablespoons finely chopped
parsley*
plain flour, to coat
cooking oil
*sliced lemon and tomato, to
garnish*

SERVES 4

Wash and clean the fish under running
water, then pat dry on kitchen paper.

Mix the garlic, cumin, salt and pepper
and parsley together and rub over the fish
inside and out. Cover and chill for 1 hour
so the fish absorbs the flavours.

Now roll each fish in the flour. Heat
enough oil in a frying pan to shallow fry
them. When it is sizzling hot, slip each fish
in and cook quickly on both sides, about
10 minutes. Serve garnished with lemon
and tomato.

Prawns in Tomato Sauce

900 g (2 lb) peeled prawns
1/2 teaspoon ground cinnamon
salt and freshly ground pepper
3 cloves garlic, crushed
2 medium onions, finely
*   chopped*
1 1/2 tablespoons oil
3 tablespoons tomato purée
5 medium ripe tomatoes, peeled,
*   chopped and puréed*
3 tablespoons lemon juice
freshly chopped parsley

SERVES 4

Season the prawns with cinnamon, salt and pepper.

Sauté the garlic and onions in the oil until they are soft. Blend in the tomato purée diluted with a little water, stirring well. Allow to simmer over a gentle heat, about 12 minutes.

Add the prawns and cook over a medium to high heat for about 10 minutes. Stir frequently and remove from heat when the prawns are tender. Sprinkle with lemon juice and parsley and serve on a bed of plain rice.

Baked Fish with Saffron Rice

*1 large whole fish (sea bass or
    sea bream), 1.75 kg (4 lb),
    gutted*

*2 cloves garlic, very finely
    chopped*

olive oil

3 tablespoons fresh lemon juice

*salt and freshly ground black
    pepper*

1 large tomato, sliced

1 lemon, sliced

*1 quantity Saffron Rice (page
    78)*

*lemon wedges and parsley, to
    garnish*

SERVES 4

Wash and clean the fish under running
water and pat it dry with kitchen paper.

Rub the fish inside and out with a
mixture of garlic, oil, lemon juice and salt
and pepper. Place the tomato and lemon
slices inside the fish and sew up with
cotton thread or skewer closed. Chill for 2
hours. Meanwhile preheat the oven to
190°C/375°F/Gas 5.

Place the fish in a large, greased
ovenproof dish and bake for 40–50
minutes until the flesh is tender and the
skin golden brown.

Serve on a bed of saffron rice and
garnish with lemon wedges and parsley.

Barbecued Fish with Dates

225 g (8 oz) dried, stoned dates

4 whole white fish, about 350 g (12 oz) each

salt and pepper

2 medium onions, finely chopped

1 clove garlic, crushed

½ teaspoon turmeric

generous pinch each of ground cumin, coriander, cardamom, nutmeg and cloves

SERVES 4

Soak the dates in cold water until they become soft, about 4 hours. Gut and rinse the fish well under cold running water. Do not scale. Dry the cavities with kitchen paper and sprinkle with a little salt and pepper.

Mix the onion, garlic and spices with a little water and stuff each fish with this mixture, sewing up the cavities, or securing with skewers.

Drain the dates, then purée in a food processor or blender with a little water, or push them through a sieve. Blend just long enough to obtain a soft paste, then smear this on both sides of each fish. Cook over a barbecue, about 5 minutes each side. Test with a fork to make sure the flesh is tender. A fish clamp is useful for the dish.

Serve hot with a rice dish. The skin together with the scales can be peeled off when eating. The date purée gives the flesh a pleasant, nutty flavour.

Fish in Hot Sauce

4 cloves garlic, chopped

*1¹/₂ teaspoons ground
  coriander*

*4 thick fillets white fish, about
  225 g (8 oz) each*

1¹/₂ tablespoons olive oil

1 tablespoon lemon juice

salt and white pepper

lemon slices, garnish

Sauce

50 g (2 oz) butter

*¹/₂ small red pepper, seeded and
  diced*

*4 medium tomatoes, skinned
  and chopped*

1 large onion, diced

1 teaspoon paprika

¹/₂ teaspoon ground ginger

pinch of salt and pepper

*1 tablespoon tomato purée
  mixed with a little water*

SERVES 4

Pound the garlic and coriander together in a pestle and mortar. Rub this into the fish fillets and chill in a covered bowl for 2 hours.

Preheat the oven to 190°C/375°F/Gas 5. Remove the fish from the bowl and rub with a mixture of the oil, lemon juice and salt and pepper. Lay the fillets in a flat, oiled ovenproof dish, cover tightly with foil and bake for 20–30 minutes, until the flesh is tender and flakes easily.

Meanwhile, prepare the sauce. Melt the butter in a pan and sauté the pepper, tomatoes and onion until soft. Add the seasonings and the tomato purée and mix well. Simmer for 10–15 minutes on a low heat.

Transfer the fish to a serving dish and garnish with the hot sauce and lemon slices.

In the Levant, fish fillets or whole fish are baked and eaten with *muhammara* (page 30) as a side dip. Some people even spread it over their fish.

Baked Fish in Tahini Sauce

*1 whole white fish, about 1.25 kg
  (2½ lb) total weight*
juice of 2 large lemons
salt and pepper
6 tablespoons olive oil
1 large onion, chopped
6 tablespoons tahini (sesame
  seed paste)
parsley, to garnish

SERVES 4

Preheat the oven to 200°C/400°F/Gas 6.
Gut, scale and clean fish under running
water. Dry, and sprinkle with some of the
lemon juice. Chill for 2 hours. Bring to
room temperature, then rub with salt and
pepper and some of the oil. Bake for 20
minutes, or until tender and the flesh
flakes easily. While the fish cooks, sauté
the onion in the remaining oil.
  Meanwhile, blend the *tahini* and

remaining lemon juice, adding water to
achieve a creamy sauce. Remove the fish
from the oven, sprinkle with the onions
and coat with *tahini* sauce. Return to the
oven and bake for a further 10 minutes.
Garnish with parsley and serve with rice
and a salad.

Tuna Shashlik

450 g (1 lb) fresh tuna
2 lemons
10 bay leaves
3 tablespoons olive oil
salt and black pepper
8 cherry tomatoes
bunch of fresh thyme
6 button onions

SERVES 4

Skin and bone the tuna and cut into chunks. Put into a bowl with the juice of 1 lemon, the bay leaves and the oil. Grind black pepper over it, mix well and marinate for 1 hour, turning frequently.

Meanwhile wash the tomatoes. Make a small incision in the tops and squeeze out the seeds. Insert a drop of oil, salt, and a few thyme leaves in each.

Slice the second lemon. Thread the fish, the onions, tomatoes, bay leaves and lemon slices alternately on to skewers. Pour the remaining marinade over them and season with salt and pepper.

Cook under a preheated hot grill for about 10 minutes. Serve immediately with *pilav* rice (page 78) and a green salad.

Stuffed Squid

6 medium squid (bodies about
    15 cm/6 inches long)
5 tablespoons olive oil
2 medium tomatoes, skinned
    and pulped
salt and pepper
pinch of paprika
juice of 1 lemon

Stuffing
2 medium onions, finely
    chopped
3 tablespoons olive oil
75 g (3 oz) rice
1 tablespoon of dill or mint,
    finely chopped
2 tablespoons parsley, finely
    chopped
1 tablespoon pine nuts
a pinch of ground cumin

SERVES 4 as a main course

To clean the squid, hold the body in one hand and gently pull off the head and arms: the innards and clear "quill" should come away as well. Clean the body thoroughly under cold running water, discarding anything left inside. Rub off any membrane from the body and set aside. Chop off the tentacles and put aside for the stuffing. Discard the heads.

In a glass bowl, mix the olive oil, the tomato pulp, salt, pepper and paprika. Place the squid bodies in this mixture, coat well and leave to marinate while you make the stuffing.

In a large pan, sauté the onions in the oil until soft. Add the chopped tentacles and cook with the onion until they change colour. Now add the rice, dill or mint, parsley, pine nuts and cumin and cook 5–10 minutes, stirring with a wooden

spoon. Leave to cool. Preheat the oven to 200C°/400°F/Gas 6.

Remove the squid from the marinade and partly fill each one with some of the stuffing. Allow room for the rice to swell during cooking. Secure the opening of each body with cocktail sticks or thread.

Arrange the squid in a lightly oiled ovenproof dish, cover with the marinade, the lemon juice and enough boiling water to almost cover them. Bake for about 50 minutes until tender. Remove and cool. Serve cold with salads.

A familiar sight throughout the Middle East is slowly turning spitted lamb, or shawarma. *The meat is often carved into a pocket of pitta bread with salad.*

Meat

My first taste of Middle Eastern cookery came in Aden, the port town on the south coast of Yemen. In 1963, a passenger liner bearing me and several hundred other young Australians called at Aden on her three-and-a-half-week voyage to Europe.

Tired of shipboard food, we streamed ashore in search of something fresh when the odour of grilling meat drew me into a small restaurant. Surrounded by curious men, I had my first taste of *kebabs*, and, while I have subsequently eaten them from Casablanca to Peshawar, I still remember this simple dish, and the cook polishing my knife and fork on his apron.

Shish kebab, to use the full name, is credited with being a Turkish creation. The story goes that Turkish soldiers, obliged to camp out during the Ottoman conquests, adopted the habit of cooking skewered meat – goat, lamb, gazelle and so on – over an open fire outside their tents. In fact, it could just as easily have been devised by invading Persian or Mongol tribes.

On the subject of *kebabs*, the most important considerations are to purchase a good cut of meat and to marinate it for at least three to four hours. I usually mix a marinade made from the juice of two large onions, 6 tablespoons olive oil, a teaspoon of oregano, a pinch of cayenne pepper, plus salt and freshly ground black pepper, and then refrigerate the meat in the mixture overnight in a covered non-metallic bowl. When barbecuing *kebabs*, or any other meat, fish or poultry, wait until the charcoal has ceased smoking before you start cooking. If using a grill, cook quickly under a high heat to seal the juices and brown the outside. The cooking time will depend on how well you like your meat done.

The ways of cooking meat in the Middle East are basically the same as in the West: grilling or barbecuing, stewing and roasting. Minced meat dishes are very popular in the Levant and Syria in particular, where women vie with each other to produce the finest *kibbeh*.

The Arabs tend to eat more barbecued meats, such as *kebabs* and lamb roasted on a spit. *Yaknéh*, or meat and vegetable stews, are common in the Levant. The Yemenis, too, are fond of stews, a popular ingredient being okra; okra *(bamieh)* is also a traditional dish in Egypt. Some Middle Eastern stews have an earthy, rather peasant-type texture – like the lamb and chick pea casserole. The more refined Persian taste, which permeates all types of local cooking, is found in the veal and prune casserole dish, a fascinating blend of "sweet and sour" ingredients.

Stews are normally simmered for a long time on the stove. Alternatively, if the ingredients have been sealed by frying or sautéeing, they are baked in the oven.

So often discarded in the West, bones are prized for the marrow, and a cracked bone is often added to stews for extra richness. Unlike meat for grilling, you can buy cheaper cuts for a stew. Searing meats in oil, or butter, traps the juices and adds a richer colour to the dish. Simmering the meat, as in many Persian recipes, makes for a light, almost insipid looking stew which is then enriched with spices, nuts and fruits. Most Middle Eastern cooks find it difficult to be precise about quantities; they tend to cook by heart with constant tastings and adjustings.

Organs are revered as we have seen with brains, liver and testicles in the chapter on *mezze*. I have marvellous memories of brains served in the Oriental buffet at the Hilton Hotel in al-Ain, the large oasis town in inland Abu Dhabi. I have eaten kidneys just about everywhere. Up early to photograph Shibam, a mountain town outside Sana'a, my driver and I had liver for breakfast. Served with a bowl of *foul* and flat wholemeal bread, it is a speciality of Yemeni mountain towns on market day.

Lamb or mutton is the most commonly used meat throughout the Middle East. Goat is also eaten by the Bedouin, and I once came upon a wedding in Abu Dhabi when a young camel had been slain and was cooking in an enormous pot of stew.

The roast, stuffed neck of lamb makes a nice change from traditional roasted Sunday lunch. Either a leg or a shoulder can be used for *kharouf bi limoun* (page 99) but I prefer a shoulder as the meat tends to be more tender. I have cooked this time and time again with unfailingly excellent results. Easily prepared, it is also a good choice if expecting guests on a week night. I serve it with boiled new potatoes liberally sprinkled with cumin, and either cold bean salad or a crisp green salad.

Of the other recipes, the okra and lamb stew recipe comes from Jordan; lamb and chick pea casserole is found throughout the Middle East (especially in Egypt when people can afford the meat); Syrian meatloaf is a useful dish – eat it hot first, then serve it cold with a salad; and I often cook *Lady's Thighs* to serve as a starter at a cocktail party. They can be made before the guests arrive and kept warm in the oven.

Levantine Lamb Stew

4 tablespoons olive oil
2 cloves garlic, crushed
1 teaspoon ground coriander
small piece of fresh ginger,
    peeled and grated
900 g (2 lb) lamb, cubed
2 medium onions, sliced
½ large lemon, cut into four
pinch of saffron or turmeric
salt and pepper, to taste
75 g (3 oz) green olives
100 g (4 oz) thick yogurt
    (optional)

SERVES 4

Heat the oil in a flameproof casserole and add the garlic, coriander, ginger and the lamb. Stir the meat in well until it is seared. Add the onions, lemon, saffron or turmeric, salt and pepper and enough water to cover.

Bring to the boil, then reduce and simmer until the lamb is tender, about 2 hours. Keep the pan covered during this time but stir the contents occasionally.

To thicken the sauce, remove the meat and allow the sauce to simmer, as desired. Strain, then stir in the olives. Stir until the sauce is as thick as you like, then return the meat to the pan and serve.

The optional addition of yogurt makes this dish even more delicious. Just before serving, stir in the yogurt and simmer, but do not boil.

Persian Casserole with Prunes

24 prunes
juice of 3 lemons
120 ml (4 fl oz) olive oil
1 teaspoon ground coriander
salt and pepper, to taste
1.5 kg (3 lb) veal, cut into cubes
3 tablespoons flaked almonds
50 g (2 oz) butter
2 medium onions, chopped
1 litre (1¾ pints) stock
1½ tablespoons icing sugar

SERVES ABOUT 6

Soak the prunes overnight.

The next day, prepare a marinade using half the lemon juice, the oil, coriander and salt and pepper. Add the meat and allow to marinate, turning once, about 2 hours. Meanwhile, preheat the oven to 180°C/350°F/Gas 4.

While the veal is marinating, toast the almonds on a baking sheet until they turn golden.

Melt the butter in a heavy-based pan and sauté the onions until soft. Drain the veal, add it to the pan and sear on all sides. Add the stock, cover and simmer on a gentle heat until tender.

Drain and stone the prunes, reserving about 300 ml (½ pint) of the juice. Mix in the icing sugar and transfer to a new pan, then simmer gently for 10–15 minutes.

Add the prune mixture, half the almonds and the remaining lemon juice to the veal. Stir well and simmer for a further 10 minutes.

Just before serving, sprinkle the remaining almonds on the top. Serve the casserole with a green salad and rice.

Roast Stuffed Neck of Lamb

*1–1.5 kg (2¼–3 lb) boned neck
    of lamb*
juice of 2 medium onions
1 tablespoon ground coriander
1 teaspoon ground ginger
*salt and freshly ground black
    pepper*
2 tablespoons oil

Stuffing
225 g (8 oz) long-grain rice
*saffron to colour, or ½
    teaspoon turmeric*
2 onions, chopped
*75 g (3 oz) pine nuts or
    blanched almonds*
½ teaspoon ground allspice
50 g (2 oz) butter
75 g (3 oz) sultanas
salt and black pepper

SERVES 4–6

Wipe the inside and outside of the neck with a cloth, rub well with onion juice, coriander, ginger and salt and pepper, then set aside.

To prepare the stuffing, cook the rice until it is light and fluffy. Sauté the onions, pine nuts and allspice in the butter, then mix with the rice. Add the sultanas, mix well and season with salt and pepper. Leave to cool.

Preheat the oven to 220°C/425°F/Gas 7. Spoon the stuffing on to the lamb and roll up. Tie with cotton string. Rub with 1 tablespoon of the oil and sear in the remaining oil in the oven.

Cook for 15 minutes, turning on all sides, then reduce the heat to 190°C/375°F/Gas 5. Roast at this heat, turn once again, then allow to become crisp. As for other lamb dishes, cooking time will depend on how you like your meat. Allow about 30 minutes per 225 g (8 oz).

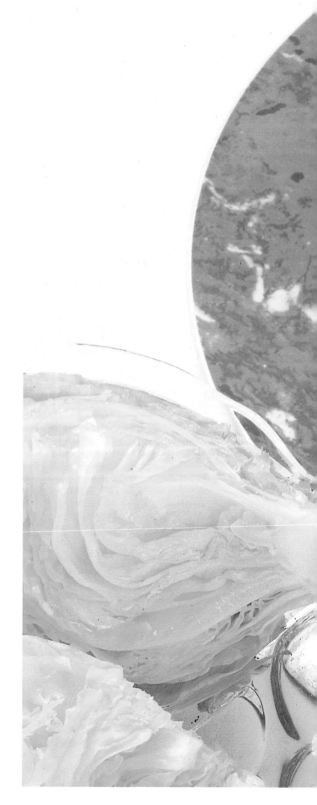

Shoulder of Lamb with Saffron

3 garlic cloves, peeled
1.25 kg (2½ lb) shoulder of
  lamb
1 teaspoon mixed herbs
salt and pepper
6 tablespoons olive oil
2 onions, sliced
juice of 2 lemons
pinch of cayenne pepper
saffron, to colour

SERVES 4

Chop the garlic into slivers and insert in small cuts all over the lamb. Mix together the herbs, salt and pepper and half the oil and marinate the lamb for 2 hours.

In a deep large frying pan, sauté the onion in the remaining oil until golden brown, then add the juice of 1 lemon. Season with cayenne pepper and simmer for 5 minutes. Remove to a large casserole. Preheat the oven to 180°C/350°F/Gas 4.

Now heat the marinade oil in the frying pan, add the shoulder and sear on all sides. Add the juice of the second lemon mixed with the saffron and transfer to the casserole. Cook until tender, 1½–2 hours.

Serve the lamb, carved into slices, garnished with sliced lemon and accompanied by rice.

Roast Leg of Lamb with Yogurt and Lemon

*1 shoulder or leg of lamb, about
  1.8 kg (4 lb)*
*salt and freshly ground black
  pepper*
4 cloves garlic
6 tablespoons olive oil
*6 tablespoons lemon juice, plus
  a little grated lemon rind*
150 ml (5 fl oz) natural yogurt

SERVES 6–8

Season the lamb well with salt and black pepper. Cut the garlic into small slivers and insert in cuts all over the leg. Set aside for 4 hours. You can use either a shoulder or a leg – a shoulder serves fewer but the meat is sweeter when it is prepared this way. Meanwhile, preheat the oven to 230°C/450°F/Gas 8.

Heat the oil in a roasting pan in the oven until it sizzles, then sear the lamb on all sides, about 15 minutes. Remove from the oven and allow to cool slightly, then pour over half the lemon juice, the rind and half the yogurt. Reduce the oven heat to about 190°C/375°F/Gas 5.

Return the lamb to the oven and roast, turning once and adding more lemon juice and yogurt. Add water if the lemon juice dries up. Do not turn after the final hour, to allow the yogurt to form a golden brown crust. The total roasting time will be about 1¾ hours.

Serve this crusty tender lamb in slices, with boiled new potatoes and cumin, and any of the green or tomato salads.

Okra and Lamb Stew

750 g (1½ lb) young okra
vinegar
3 cloves garlic, crushed
2 onions, chopped
1 teaspoon ground coriander
1½ tablespoons butter
900 g (2 lb) lean lamb, cubed
6 medium ripe tomatoes, or
   275 g (10 oz) can with juice,
   chopped
350 ml (12 fl oz) meat stock
salt and freshly ground black
   pepper
1½ tablespoons lemon juice

SERVES 4–5

Wash the okra and cut off the stems, taking care not to puncture the pods. Soak pods in vinegar for 30 minutes, then drain and dry on kitchen paper.

Sauté the garlic, onion and coriander in the butter in a large saucepan or flameproof casserole, then add the lamb and seal over a high heat. Turn each piece until it changes colour, then add the okra and tomatoes. Simmer for 5–10 minutes, then cover with the stock. Season with salt and pepper, stir well, and simmer over a low heat for 1½–2 hours, or until tender. By this time the sauce should be greatly reduced. Add the lemon juice just before serving.

Lamb and Chick Pea Casserole

225 g (8 oz) dried chick peas
1 large onion, chopped
4 cloves garlic, finely chopped
1 teaspoon ground allspice
1 teaspoon paprika
pinch of ground coriander
salt and freshly ground black pepper
5 tablespoons olive oil
900 g (2 lb) boned lamb, cut into pieces
1 shin bone with marrow, chopped into 2 or 3 pieces
600 ml (1 pint) water
2 small aubergines
1½ tablespoons lemon juice
6 tablespoons tahini (sesame seed paste)

SERVES 4

Soak the chick peas overnight in cold water. The next day, drain.

Sauté the onion, garlic and seasonings in half the oil. Add the pieces of lamb and brown quickly on all sides.

Place the meat and onion mixture, the marrow bones and water into a deep, heavy-based flameproof casserole and simmer over a low heat, stirring occasionally, until tender.

Remove the casserole from the heat and allow the mixture to cool. Take out the bones and extract the marrow, dropping it into the stew. Set aside while you prepare the aubergines.

Thinly slice the aubergines, lay the pieces on a wooden board and sprinkle with salt. Leave for 1 hour, then rinse under cold running water and pat dry on kitchen paper.

Fry the aubergine in the remaining oil. Drain well on kitchen paper and keep warm.

Skim off any fat which has settled on the casserole, add salt and pepper and blend in the lemon juice and *tahini* paste.

Stir in well, add the slices of aubergines and keep in a warm oven until ready to serve. Serve with pitta bread to mop up the rich sauce, and a potato salad.

Braised Chops with Vegetables

courgettes or leeks (or other
    vegetables), see recipe
8–10 fleshy lamb chops
1½ tablespoons butter
1 large onion, sliced
2–3 cloves garlic, chopped
generous pinch of ground
    coriander, paprika and
    ground allspice
6 medium ripe tomatoes, sliced
2 tablespoons finely chopped
    parsley
salt and freshly ground black
    pepper
175 ml (6 fl oz) stock

SERVES 4

Use 2 large courgettes or about 450 g
(1 lb) leeks.

Trim the chops of any excess fat and
brown in butter on both sides. Remove
from the frying pan and place in a greased
ovenproof dish. Preheat the oven to
190°C/375°F/Gas 5.

Sauté the onion, garlic and spices in the
butter remaining in the frying pan until
softened. Add the tomatoes, half the
parsley and salt and pepper. Simmer for
10 minutes, then add the stock, stirring
thoroughly.

Place the sliced vegetables on top of the
chops, and pour the sauce mixture over
them. Add more seasoning, as desired.

Cook in the oven until the chops are
tender and the sauce is rich and aromatic.
Garnish with the remaining parsley. Serve
with mashed or baked potatoes, slashed
open, and garnished with butter and
cumin.

Meatballs in Yogurt Sauce

75 g (3 oz) bulghur *(cracked wheat), soaked and dried*

900 g (2 lb) lean minced beef

pinch of paprika and ground allspice

salt and freshly ground pepper

3 medium onions, very finely chopped

50 g (2 oz) pine nuts

1½ tablespoons butter

cooking oil

Yogurt sauce

200 ml (7 fl oz) natural yogurt

1 tablespoon cornflour

salt and pepper, to taste

2–3 cloves garlic, crushed

2 tablespoons dried mint, crushed

butter for frying

SERVES 4

Wash the *bulghur* and soak in cold water for 2 hours. Squeeze dry in a clean tea-towel. Mix together the meat, *bulghur* and spices, and mix to a paste-like consistency. Meanwhile sauté the onions and pine nuts lightly in the butter and allow to cool.

Break off lumps of meat the size of a golf ball and stuff with the pine nut and onion mixture. Heat the oil in a deep saucepan and fry the meatballs until crisp on the outside, but juicy within. Drain on kitchen paper and keep warm.

To stabilize the yogurt, pour it into a large saucepan and beat until liquid. Mix the cornflour with a little water to make a paste. Add this to the yogurt together with a pinch of salt. Heat to just below boiling while stirring continuously in one direction. Continue to stir the mixture over a minimum heat, or until the sauce thickens. Do not cover, or over-heat.

Sauté the garlic in a little butter, add the mint and mix this into the yogurt sauce. Season further according to taste.

Place the meatballs in a serving dish and cover with the sauce. Serve with plain rice and chopped Arab salad, with pitta bread to mop up the sauce.

Syrian Stuffed Kibbeh

75 g (3 oz) bulghur (cracked
  wheat)
2 medium onions
450 g (1lb) minced beef
generous pinch of paprika
salt and freshly ground black
  pepper
cayenne pepper, to taste

Filling
1 medium onion, finely
  chopped
25 g (1 oz) pine nuts
about 50 g (2 oz) butter
225 g (8 oz) finely minced lamb
1/2 teaspoon ground allspice
salt and freshly ground black
  pepper

SERVES 4

Make the *kibbeh* mixture first. Wash the *bulghur* and soak in cold water for 2 hours. Squeeze dry in a clean tea-towel.

Grate the onion in a food processor, then add the meat and seasonings, and mix to a paste-like consistency.

To make the filling, sauté the onion and pine nuts in the butter. When they turn golden brown, add the meat and allspice to the pan, cooking lightly until the meat changes colour. Add salt and pepper and mix well. While this cools, prepare the *kibbeh* shells.

Break off a lump the size of a small egg, and cupping in it in your palm, make a hole in the centre with your finger. Mould the paste around your finger, working up and down and round and round (a practice likened by Middle Eastern cookery expert, Claudia Roden, to pottery making). It is a difficult art: if the paste breaks, use moistened hands to stick it together again.

Now fill each egg-shaped *kibbeh* with a little stuffing. Seal the edges by wetting with iced water. As each *kibbeh* is made, set it aside on a tray (you can prepare them in advance and chill them).

Heat a deep frying pan with enough oil to cover the *kibbeh*. When the oil is sizzling, drop them in and cook on a high heat, turning frequently until they turn rich brown but the filling remains juicy. Drain on kitchen paper and serve either hot or cold, with a selection of dips and salads.

The Syrians are masters at making kibbeh, *the pounding of the mince and* bulghur *being a familiar sound. Pictured here are stuffed* kibbeh *served with* hummus *(page 26) and* muhammara *(page 30) dips and pitta bread.*

Ground Meat Kebabs

*900 g (2 lb) lean minced beef or
   lamb*

*3 medium onions, finely
   chopped*

*6 tablespoons coarsely chopped
   parsley*

*salt and freshly ground black
   pepper*

½ teaspoon ground allspice

½ teaspoon cayenne papper

flour for dusting

oil for brushing

SERVES 6

Light the barbecue (if using) or preheat
the grill. Put the meat and the reminaing
ingredients, except the flour and oil, into a
food processor and work together.

With moistened hands, break off
walnut-sized lumps of the mixture and
mould into sausage shapes around a
skewer (2 per skewer). You should fill 6
skewers in all. Dust with flour to hold
firmly, then brush lightly with oil and cook
over the barbecue or under the grill,
turning frequently.

Serve on a platter lined with lettuce,
garnished with lemon wedges and
hummus or *muhammara*.

Turkish-style Kebabs

900 g (2 lb) lean meat (see recipe)

salt and pepper, to taste

juice of 2 lemons

4 tablespoons olive oil

1 teaspoon chopped marjoran

paprika (optional)

1 red or green pepper

2 onions

2 firm tomatoes

4 kidneys, cored and trimmed (optional)

SERVES 4

Choose a lean piece of lamb or beef, and cut into chunky cubes. Rub with salt and freshly ground black pepper and marinate in lemon juice, olive oil and marjoram for about 2 hours. (To make the *kebabs* more piquant, add a good pinch of paprika to the marinade.)

Cut up chunks of green or red pepper, onions and firm tomatoes to intersperse with the meat. Cored and halved kidneys are also delicious.

Spear the meat, onions, tomato and chunks of pepper alternately on 8 skewers, then cook under a preheated grill, turning frequently until they are cooked on all sides. Serve 2 skewers per person.

Syrian Meatloaf

50 g (2 oz) pine nuts

2 tablespoons butter, diced

2 egg yolks

2 medium onions, finely chopped

3 tablespons tomato purée

1 teaspoon ground allspice

5 cm (2 inch) piece of fresh ginger, peeled and grated

salt and freshly ground black pepper

900 g (2 lb) lean minced lamb

50 g (2 oz) fresh breadcrumbs

lemon wedges and cress or parsley, to garnish

SERVES 6–8

First sauté the pine nuts lightly in a little butter and set aside. Preheat the oven to 190°C/375°F/Gas 5.

In a mixing bowl beat the egg yolks, then add the onions, tomato purée, allspice, ginger and salt and pepper. Mix together well.

Knead the lamb thoroughly in a mixing bowl. Make a hollow in the centre, pour in the egg mixture, add the pine nuts and mix well. Finally add the fresh breadcrumbs to bind the mixture. Form into a loaf shape, and spinkle with a little cold water and dot with the remaining butter. Wrap in foil and bake for 1–1½ hours, unwrapping the foil for the final 30 minutes to allow to brown.

Syrian meatloaf may be served either hot or cold. This recipe leaves enough over to use cold; it is a good picnic dish. Serve with side dishes of *labneh* (page 28) and salad.

Kidneys in Tomato Sauce

12 lambs' kidneys
lemon juice or vinegar
2 onions, finely chopped
2 cloves garlic, crushed
pinch each of chilli powder,
  ground coriander, ground
  cumin and chopped parsley
1½ tablespoons butter
4 medium tomatoes, skinned
  and pulped
1 tablespoon tomato purée
salt and freshly ground black
  pepper

SERVES 4

Soak the kidneys in water with 2 teaspoons of lemon juice or vinegar for about 2 hours. Drain, skin, slice in half and remove the cores. Cut into quarters.

Sauté the onion, garlic and seasonings in the butter. Add the kidneys and toss lightly until they change colour. Add the tomato pulp and purée, mixing well. Finally add the salt and pepper and 1–2 tablespoons water.

Cook gently on a low heat, about 10–15 minutes, according to how you like kidneys done. Serve with plain rice, pitta bread and a green salad.

Pigeon is a great delicacy in the Middle East. Here a girl collects eggs in al-Fayyoum Oasis.

Poultry

One medieval Middle Eastern recipe book lists over 300 different ways of cooking poultry, especially chicken. Apparently Kaskari chickens (Kaskar is a village between the Tigris and the Euphrates) were considered to have the best taste and, according to one translator, they grew "as heavy as a goat, or a sheep." The breeding of chickens appears to have been common at this time, yet it was not so long ago, especially in the Arab countries, that chickens were so scarce they were considered a luxury.

I recall an incident during travels through Yemen when, invited to eat at a rural dwelling, I was sitting and talking to my host. A terrible squawking came from below and peering out a window, I saw a boy chasing a scraggy hen until, with a well aimed stick, he killed it. The fact that it was his father's only chicken underlined the family's incredible hospitality. Now ironically, like most Middle Eastern towns, even the capital Sana'a has a "Kentucky Fried Chicken" take-away (although it was closed for months as the owner was rumoured to be a Jew!)

It is probably true that there are more ways of cooking poultry than any other ingredient in the Middle Eastern repertoire. Recipes in this chapter range from chicken *kebab* to the exotic duck in walnut and pomegranate sauce. Finding we were only two one Christmas, I cooked Persian chicken (stuffed with apricots, prunes, raisins and pine nuts) which was as good as, and much more economical than, the traditional English turkey.

There is a delicious recipe for lemon chicken (although it makes a mess of the grill pan). I serve it hot with a green side salad, but it is equally good cold. I once made it my basic dish for a picnic to watch the Oxford and Cambridge boat race: it poured with rain and the Cambridge crew sank – but my lemon chicken dish saved the day!

The recipe for chicken casseroled with lemon juice was supplied by the Holiday Inn in Amman. Easy to prepare, it can be made in advance for a dinner party.

Ferakh al-hara (hot chicken) is one of the easiest dishes to make in the book, an ideal recipe should you be eating alone after a busy day at work. I have a very "seasoned" palate, liking things hot, and tend to substitute chilli powder for the sweeter paprika.

Cafés in Amman, Jericho and Jersualem are known for chicken *musakhan*, a take-away snack like *döner kebap*, or *shawarma* as it is known in Arabic. *Sumaka*, a red spice with a lemony tang, gives it the characteristic flavour, but this is difficult to buy in Britain.

As well as being masters at cooking chickens in so many different ways, Middle Eastern cooks take great pains to ensure that each dish has special eye appeal. Beautifully garnished with red paprika in oil and chopped walnuts, Circassian chicken is a good example. Side dishes are fluffy white rice and an emerald-green salad.

Fesanjan, or tender duck steeped in walnuts and pomegranates, is the king of all the poultry dishes. The medieval Persian recipe conjures up all the pomp and pageantry of the glorious reign of the Safavid *shahs*. If you can't find fresh pomegranates, use lemon juice or pomegranate juice concentrate, but the appearance of the dish will obviously suffer.

Restaurants in Lebanon have traditionally served small birds as *mezze*. Rubbed with salt, pepper and olive oil, they are grilled on skewers over a charcoal fire. A restaurant in the mountain town of Bhamdoun was famous for birds served in this manner. In Egypt, migrating quail are netted near Agami, a popular beach resort with Cairo's élite near Alexandria. Pigeons are kept by many families – elaborately built pigeon lofts are a feature in al-Fayyoum Oasis, near Cairo. Syrian farmers, especially around Aleppo, breed pigeons for the family pot.

Lemon Chicken Casserole

*1 × 1.5 kg (3 lb) chicken, or 2
    small chickens*
*about 6 tablespoons lemon
    juice, plus extra for cooking*
3 medium onions, chopped
3 cloves garlic, crushed
salt and pepper
pinch of paprika
1½–2 tablespoons butter
parsley, to garnish

SERVES 4–5

Skin and bone the chicken, then cut the
flesh into cubes.

Make a marinade of the lemon juice,
onions, garlic, salt and pepper and
paprika. Add the chicken, stir well, cover
and chill for 4–6 hours.

Remove the chicken from the marinade
and pat dry. Sauté the chicken in the butter
in a deep pan, adding 225 ml (8 fl oz)
water and lemon juice to taste.

Cover and simmer over a low heat until
tender, 30–40 minutes. Serve with saffron
rice (page 78), garnished with extra
paprika and parsley.

Chicken in Yogurt

75 g (3 oz) butter
2 medium onions, sliced
1 × 1.25–1.5 kg (2½–3 lb)
   chicken, cut into 8 pieces
pinch of salt
freshly ground black pepper
300 ml (½ pint) chicken stock
75 ml (3 fl oz) single cream
75 ml (3 fl oz) natural yogurt
juice of 1–2 lemons

SERVES 4

Melt the butter in frying pan and sauté the onions until they are soft and translucent. Add the chicken and quickly brown on all sides, about 10 minutes over a medium heat.

Add the seasonings and stock and simmer uncovered for about 30 minutes, turning occasionally. Meanwhile, preheat the oven to 190°C/375°F/Gas 5.

Mix together the cream, yogurt and lemon juice to taste.

Grease a casserole, transfer the chicken to it and pour the creamy sauce over. Roast about 1½ hours, or until the chicken is tender and the juices run clear if the flesh is pierced with the tip of a knife. Turn occasionally and add more lemon juice mixed with water if too much sauce evaporates. Serve with mashed potatoes, a green salad and bread for mopping up the rich, unctuous sauce.

Chicken Musakhan

1 × 900 g (2 lb) chicken, cut into
    4 pieces
450 ml (¾ pint) chicken stock
1 small celery stalk with leaves
1 medium onion, sliced
salt and pepper
4 small onions sliced into fine
    rings
1 tablespoon pine nuts
3 tablespoons oil
4 pitta breads
2 teaspoons sumak (if available)

SERVES 4

Place the chicken pieces in a casserole, cover with the stock and add the celery, the sliced onion and salt and pepper. Cover and simmer until tender, about 40 minutes. Remove the chicken and set aside a little of the stock. While the chicken is cooking, sauté the onion rings and pine nuts in the oil.

Arrange the bread on the grill tray and top each piece with a portion of chicken, some of the onion rings and dribble a little stock over them. Sprinkle each with *sumak* and grill until the chicken turns golden brown. Take care not to burn the bread. Serve garnished with pine nuts and extra onion rings.

Musakhan can be eaten by itself, or with a salad. It is a novel ideal for lunch in the garden.

Circassian Chicken

1 × 1.5 kg (3 lb) chicken
1 large onion, chopped
1 clove garlic, chopped
2 celery sticks, chopped
salt and freshly ground black
    pepper
350 g (12 oz) long-grain rice
90 g (3½ oz) walnuts, finely
    chopped
2 tablespoons olive oil
1 teaspoon paprika

SERVES 4–5

Put the chicken, onion, garlic, celery and salt and pepper in a large saucepan, cover with water and simmer until tender, about 1½ hours. Remove and drain the chicken (reserving the stock), and keep warm in a low oven.

Chill the stock quickly, then skim as much fat as possible off the surface.

Cook the rice (see page 78), and keep warm in a low oven.

Meanwhile make the sauce. Put the walnuts in a deep frying pan with 175 ml

(6 fl oz) of the reserved cooking stock. Simmer, stirring until the mixture thickens. Season with salt and pepper.

Now blend the oil and the paprika together until the oil becomes bright red. Cut the chicken into attractive serving portions, arrange them in a serving dish. Cover with the sauce and trickle the red oil on top.

Ferakh al-hara Hot chicken

5 tablespoons olive oil
juice of 1 lemon
1 teaspoon chilli powder, to taste
salt and pepper
1 heaped teaspoon crushed
   garlic
1 × 900 g (2 lb) chicken, cut into
   4 pieces
lemon wedges, to garnish

SERVES 4

Preheat the oven to 190°C/375°F/Gas 5.
Mix together the oil, lemon juice, chilli
powder, salt, pepper and garlic in a bowl.
   Place the chicken pieces in an
ovenproof dish and cover with the
mixture. Bake for 40 minutes, basting
occasionally. Do not baste for the final
15–20 minutes to allow the chicken to
become crisp.
   Serve with pilav rice (page 78) and salad
or as desired. Garnish with lemon wedges.

116

Persian Chicken

*2 medium onions, finely
   chopped*

100 g (4 oz) butter

40 g (1½ oz) raisins

*175 g (6 oz) dried prunes,
   soaked, stoned and sliced*

*175 g (6 oz) dried apricots,
   soaked and sliced*

1 teaspoon ground cinnamon

*salt and freshly ground black
   pepper*

1 × 1.5 kg (3 lb) chicken

SERVES 4

Sauté the onion in half the butter for a few minutes, then add the raisins, prunes and apricots and sauté gently for a further 5 minutes. Season the mixture with cinnamon, salt and pepper, and allow to cool.

Preheat the oven to 190°C/375°F/Gas 5. Stuff the chicken with the fruit mixture. Sew up the neck flap to keep the moisture in. Rub all over with salt, pepper and remaining butter, then wrap in foil and bake in the oven.

Open the foil after 40 minutes so the skin will brown and become crisp. The total cooking time is approximately 1½ hours.

Roast Chicken Stuffed with Rice and Pine Nuts

1 large onion, finely chopped
100 g (4 oz) butter, melted
*75 g (3 oz) chicken livers,
    trimmed and minced*
100 g (4 oz) sausagemeat
100 g (4 oz) rice
50 g (2 oz) pine nuts
½ teaspoon ground cinnamon
¼ teaspoon ground allspice
*salt and freshly ground black
    pepper*
225 ml (8 fl oz) chicken stock
1 × 1.5 kg (3 lb) chicken

SERVES 4

Using a deep frying pan, sauté the onion in two-thirds of the melted butter until it turns soft and golden. Add the liver and sausagemeat and stir-fry until lightly brown. Next add the rice, pine nuts, cinnamon, allspice and salt and pepper and cook about 5 minutes. To this add the stock and cook over a low heat until it is absorbed, 12–15 minutes. Allow to cool. Preheat the oven to 190°C/375°F/Gas 5.

Rub the entire chicken with salt and pepper. Spoon in the stuffing and close the openings with either small skewers or thread.

Brush with remaining melted butter and roast until the chicken is crisp and tender, about 2 hours. To crisp the skin, do not baste for the last 30 minutes.

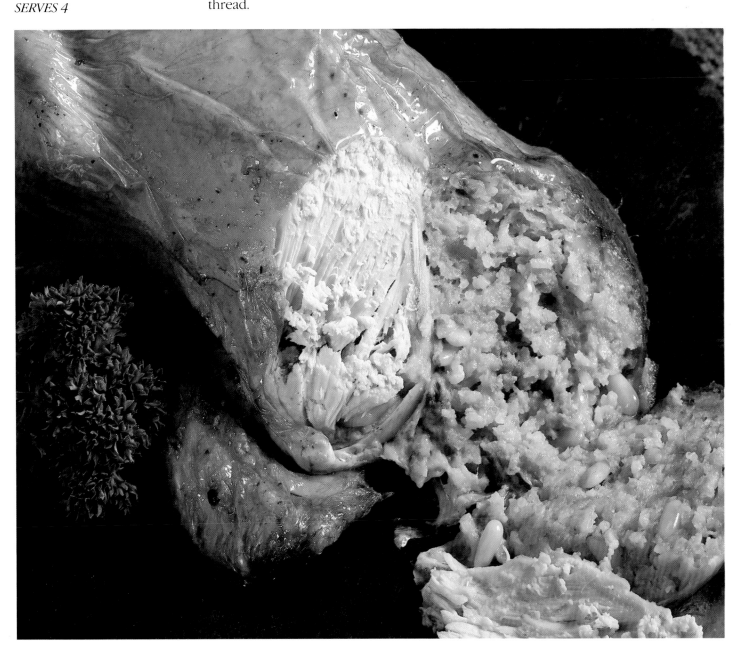

Chicken Kebabs

*1 × 1.25 kg (2½ lb) chicken,
   boned and cut into good
   sized cubes (see recipe)*
6 tablespoons olive oil
6 tablespoons lemon juice
2 cloves garlic, crushed
*salt and freshly ground black
   pepper*
*saffron to colour, or ½
   teaspoon turmeric*
1 tablespoon melted butter

SERVES 4

A barbecue is ideal for cooking these chicken *kebabs*, but a good grill is perfectly adequate. The chicken pieces should be of a size that will stay firmly on the skewers (leaving the skin on helps). Combine the oil, lemon juice, garlic, and salt and pepper in a bowl, and place the chicken cubes in it. Cover and marinate for several hours, turning occasionally. Preheat the grill or light the barbecue.

Dissolve the saffron or turmeric in the melted butter. Thread the chicken pieces on to the skewers and brush with this mixture. Cook over or under a high heat, turning and basting frequently with the butter, for about 15 minutes.

Serve the *kebabs* on the skewers on a bed of saffron rice (page 78), garnished with sliced oranges. A plain green salad would complement the meal nicely.

Grilled Lemon Chicken

1 large onion, very finely chopped
juice of 2 large lemons
5 tablespoons peanut butter
175 ml (6 fl oz) olive oil
salt, to taste
freshly ground black pepper
2 × 900 g (2 lb) chickens, each cut into 6 pieces

SERVES 6

Mix together the onion, lemon juice, peanut butter, oil and salt and pepper and brush on the chicken pieces. Place under a medium-hot grill and cook until tender. Turn the pieces and baste frequently with the mixture, watching that it does not burn. Serve when golden brown and tender and the juices are clear if the chicken is pierced with the tip of a knife.

The chicken pieces may be eaten hot, or cold, with a lettuce salad, rice and pitta bread.

Chicken with Olives

350 g (12 oz) green olives,
stoned and chopped

salt and pepper

3 cloves garlic, crushed

2 tablespoons olive oil

1 teaspoon grated fresh ginger

2–3 strands of saffron

1 chicken, about 1.5 kg (3 lb),
cut into 8 pieces

350 ml (12 fl oz) chicken stock

1 teaspoon paprika

1 teaspoon ground cumin

6 tablespoons lemon juice

SERVES 4

Bring the chopped olives to the boil 3 times in a deep saucepan. Change the water each time, the last time using 300 ml (½ pint) water with a pinch of salt. Remove from the stove and press the olives down with a potato masher to extract more juices. Set aside.

Sauté the garlic in the oil in a large, deep frying pan. Add the ginger, saffron, chicken pieces and the stock. Cover and cook slowly over a medium heat, turning at intervals, 30–40 minutes.

When the chicken is tender and the juices run clear, remove it from the pan and keep warm. Now reduce the broth until it becomes thick and pungent. Add the paprika, cumin, lemon juice and more salt and pepper according to taste. Simmer for a minute, then add the olives and their juices, stir well and allow the sauce to further thicken, 12–15 minutes.

When ready to serve, return the chicken portions to the pan and heat through in the sauce. Serve each portion garnished with olives, with pitta bread to mop up the sauce, *pilav* rice (page 78) and chopped salad.

Duck in Walnut and Pomegranate Sauce

2 medium onions, chopped

1½ tablespoons melted clarified butter

150 g (5 oz) brown sugar

1 teaspoon ground cinnamon

9 tablespoons pomegranate juice (about 3 fruits) or use grenadine syrup

450 ml (15 fl oz) home-made stock

1 duck, about 1.8 kg (4 lb)

salt and black pepper

100 g (4 oz) chopped walnuts

Garnish (optional)
100 g (4 oz) chopped walnuts
seeds of 2 pomegranates

SERVES 4

Preheat the oven to 190°C/375°F/Gas 4. Sauté the onions in the melted butter until soft and transparent. Add the sugar, cinnamon, pomegranate juice and stock and stir well. Simmer over a medium heat for about 10 minutes.

Rub the duck with salt and pepper, increase the oven temperature to 200°C/400°F/Gas 6 and cook for 15 minutes. Remove and drain off any fat.

Spoon the pomegranate sauce over the duck, return to the oven at 180°C/350°F/Gas 4 and continue roasting. Drain off the fat and turn and baste as necessary. Do not turn again for the final 1 hour of roasting.

When the duck is almost tender, add the chopped walnuts to the remaining sauce, in the pan, adjust seasoning to taste, stir and simmer on a low heat. Set aside and keep warm.

Options when serving are to present the duck whole, garnished with the rest of the sauce, chopped walnuts and pomegranate seeds, or to carve and pour the sauce over each portion. You can also put the remaining sauce in a gravy boat for people to help themselves. Serve with *pilau* rice (page 78) and a green salad.

The aroma of these freshly baked biscuits wafts through the market in Manama, Bahrain.

Desserts and Sweetmeats

The oldest known Islamic sweetmeat is *faludhaj*, a Persian concoction of ground almonds, sugar, rose water and other ingredients, which is believed to have been introduced in Mecca to cater for pilgrims making the *haj* or pilgrimage.

Ancient Arab and Farsi records make little reference to other rich desserts, but the Muslim sweet tooth can be traced back at least as far as the Abbasid caliphate. Recipe books from this period indicate that Abbasid society was addicted to sweetmeats, a taste not restricted to affluent families.

Among a variety of rich sweetmeats were *lawzinia* (a confection of almonds, breadcrumbs and syrup), *zalabiya* (an almond and rose water-flavoured tart) and *khabis*, which seems to have been a gelatine-like dessert made with breadcrumbs, milk, sugar and sesame seed oil. Sugar, honey, molasses and syrup were commonly used sweeteners. Many people in the Middle East still believe that eating honey and other sweet things will ward off the "evil eye".

Sweets figure in many prominent dates in the Muslim calendar. Prior to *Muharram* (the first ten days of the New Year) or on the Prophet's birthday, housewives are busy baking traditional sweetmeats. It is a custom to take these to relatives and friends who similarly call with their own home-made specialities.

Baklava is probably the best-known sweetmeat. I have eaten *baklava* in places as far apart as Dakar and Sydney – wherever there are Lebanese, Turkish or Armenian migrants. The Greeks also claim it is their own invention, but its true origins are obscure. *Baklava* is best eaten within a day or two of preparation. It can be made using either walnuts or pistachio nuts.

Basbousa is another syrupy sweetmeat which can be made with yogurt or coconut. It may be eaten hot or cold, with or without cream. There is a horrible little shop just outside Baalbek, in Jordan, which makes quite the best *basbousa* in the Middle East.

There can be few people who have never tasted *lokum*, or Turkish Delight as it is more commonly known. Many restaurants habitually offer a dish with coffee. I have not supplied a recipe for Turkish Delight as it can be readily bought and it is *so* time consuming to prepare. Also served with coffee are delicate almond fingers, a truly magical sweetmeat which I have enjoyed in many Middle Eastern homes.

Ma'moul are bite-sized pastries of many different shapes and fillings. Outside the Great Ummayad Mosque in Damascus is a shop selling them oven-warm. You can buy a bag for less than a pound to eat as you wander through the bazaar, one of the biggest and most interesting in the Middle East.

Dates have a myriad uses in Middle Eastern cookery. The Bedouin often eat them with bread and yogurt as a substantial meal. They can be stuffed with marzipan or puréed to give a nutty flavour to fish. Tribes in remote parts of Saudi Arabia sustain their camels on date meal.

While the Palestinian town of Jericho is more famous for citrus fruits, bananas also flourish in the almost semi-tropical climate of the Jordan Valley trench. Plantations can be seen on either side of the River Jordan, and after the harvest, bananas hang side by side with oranges and grapefruit in Jericho's roadside stalls. Banana cake or banana loaf is an old Palestinian recipe, sometimes sold in shops, more often made at home.

Recipes appear for three glorious Middle Eastern desserts. My own favourite, *ma'mounia* or "Caliph's Delight", is a recipe said to have been created for the Caliph Ma'moun. A speciality of the Syrian town of Aleppo, it is often eaten for breakfast smothered in cream. Local folklore says it assists a woman to regain her strength after childbirth – what it does for men being something of a moot point. Similar to the drier *basbousa*, which is also made from farina, *ma'mounia* is extravagantly rich.

Made from ground rice, *muhallabia* is to the Middle East what rice pudding is to England or America. A very simple, delicately flavoured dish, it is eaten throughout the region, then under the name of *firni*, it pops up in Pakistan having probably been introduced by the Mughal emperors.

Umm Ali, or "Mother of Ali", is a very rich pudding, very fattening and utterly irresistible if you have a sweet tooth. Dried fruit salad can be made with many different combinations of dried fruits and nuts. It is served when Muslims break the fast at dusk. Eat it with cream and be sure to make enough to have on breakfast cereal – it's alsolutely delicious.

"Caliph's Delight"

450 ml (¾ pint) water
juice of 1 lemon
300 g (10 oz) white sugar
100 g (4 oz) butter
25 g (1 oz) pine nuts, chopped
100 g (4 oz) semolina
300 ml (½ pint) clotted cream
ground cinnamon, to sprinkle

SERVES 6

Combine the water, lemon juice and sugar in a saucepan, bring to the boil and simmer for 15 minutes.

In a large frying pan, melt the butter and lightly sauté the pine nuts. Add the semolina and cook on a low heat until the semolina turns light brown, about 5 minutes.

Remove from the heat and stir in the syrup. Return to a low heat, stir well and cook for a further 5 minutes. Transfer the mixture to a serving dish. Smooth the cream over the mixture. Sprinkle with cinnamon and serve.

Umm Ali   "Mother of Ali"

275 g (10 oz) cooked puff pastry

50 g (2 oz) pistachio nuts, chopped

50 g (2 oz) flaked almonds, toasted

1½ teaspoons lemon juice

250 ml (8 fl oz) milk

175 g (6 oz) sugar

a pinch of cinnamon

1 egg, beaten

2 teaspoons rose water

250 ml (8 fl oz) single cream

SERVES 6

Preheat the oven to 190°C/375°F/Gas 5. Grease a round, glass ovenproof dish, and crumble the pastry into the dish. Mix in the nuts and lemon juice.

Heat the milk, sugar and cinnamon to just below boiling point, then slowly add the beaten egg. Pour this over the pastry mixture in the dish, and sprinkle with rose water. Top with the cream and bake for about 30 minutes, until golden.

Muhallabia   Ground rice pudding

1.2 litres (2 pints) milk
3 tablespoons ground rice
1 tablespoon cornflour
6 tablespoons sugar
1 tablespoon rose water
100 g (4 oz) ground almonds
flaked blanched almonds or
  pistachio nuts, to garnish
grated nutmeg, to sprinkle

SERVES 6

With a little of the milk, mix the ground rice and cornflour to a smooth paste.

Slowly heat the sugar in the rest of the milk, and add the rice paste, stirring continuously with a wooden spoon. Simmer the mixture until just below boiling point, and take care not to let it burn on the bottom as this will spoil the delicate flavour. The mixture should thicken in about 15 minutes.

Add the rose water and ground almonds and continue stirring in one direction on a low heat. Simmer for a further 5 minutes, then remove from the heat and cool slightly before pouring the mixture into an attractive glass blowl, or individual glass dishes.

Garnish with almonds or pistachio nuts, and sprinkle with the nutmeg. Leave to chill for about 3–4 hours before serving.

Banana Loaf

100 g (4 oz) butter, softened
3½ tablespoons sugar
2 eggs
pinch of cinnamon
1 teaspoon vanilla essence
3 medium ripe bananas
25 g (1 oz) walnuts, coarsely
  chopped
150 g (5 oz) plain flour
2 teaspoons baking powder
1 teaspoon bicarbonate of soda
pinch of salt
1 tablespoon milk

Preheat the oven to 180°C/350°F/Gas 5.
Line a 23 cm (9 inch) loaf tin with greased
greaseproof paper.

Cream the butter and sugar together,
then add the eggs, one at a time, beating
after each addition. Add the cinnamon and
vanilla and beat well.

Mash the bananas to a pulp, then stir
into the mixture together with the
walnuts. Combine well, then fold in the
sifted dry ingredients, alternating with the
milk. Pour the mixture into the tin. Bake
for 50–60 minutes until a skewer comes
out clean. Turn out on to a wire rack, peel
off the lining paper and leave to cool.

Date Rolls

120 g (4½ oz) plain flour
200 g (7 oz) unsalted butter,
softened
1 tablespoon icing sugar
1 tablespoon oil
1½ tablespoons milk
icing sugar for dusting

Filling
1½ tablespoons butter
1½ tablespoons water
350 g (12 oz) dates, stoned and
chopped

MAKES ABOUT 24

Make the filling first. Melt the butter together with the water in a saucepan, then add the chopped dates. Cook over a low heat, stirring the dates and pressing down until they become a soft paste. Remove and cool.

To make the dough, sift the flour into a mixing bowl. Cut the soft butter into small pieces and work it into the flour with your fingers. Add the sugar and mix in thoroughly. Make a well in the centre, pour in the oil and milk, then continue to knead the dough until pieces flake off the sides of the bowl. Knead a further 10 minutes, then roll into a ball and chill.

Meanwhile, preheat the oven to 180°C/350°F/Gas 4. Grease a large baking tray. Remove the dough from the refrigerator and divide into 3 portions. Knead each well.

On a floured board, roll out and flatten a ball of dough. Cut into a neat rectangle shape. Spread one-third of the date mixture thinly over the top. Roll the rectangle into a sausage shape and continue to roll backwards and forwards until it grows longer and thinner. Slice this into flattened rounds about 4 cm (1½ inch) thick. Repeat this process using the remaining balls of dough.

Place all the slices side by side on the greased baking sheet and prick the tops lightly with a fork. Bake for 25–30 minutes until slightly coloured (if you overcook them, they become hard). Allow to cool, then dust with icing sugar.

Baklava

About 20 sheets filo pastry, thawed if frozen

225 g (8 oz) unsalted butter, melted and clarified

225 g (8 oz) chopped pistachio nuts or walnuts

1 teaspoon ground cinnamon

75 g (3 oz) sugar

Syrup

225 g (8 oz) sugar

125 ml (4 fl oz) water

1 tablespoon lemon juice

1 tablespoon orange flower water

Make the syrup first to give it time to chill. Dissolve all the ingredients together over a medium heat. Remove from the stove when the mixture thickens enough to coat a spoon, then cool and chill thoroughly. Meanwhile, preheat the oven to 180°C/350°F/Gas 4.

Grease a rectangular ovenproof dish that is 30 × 20 cm (12 × 8 inches). Lay 9 of the sheets of filo in the dish, brushing the top of each with melted butter as it is laid down.

Mix together the nuts, cinnamon and sugar and spread half over the top filo sheet. Place 2 more buttered sheets on top, and cover with the rest of the nut mixture. Layer up the remaining filo sheets, brushing each with butter as before. With a sharp knife, cut a diamond pattern in the top. Sprinkle with water to prevent the top layers of pastry from curling.

Bake for 30 minutes, then increase the oven temperature to 220°C/425°F/Gas 7. Bake for a further 10–15 minutes, until the pastry is puffy and the top is gold. If the top layer cooks too quickly, cover it with foil, but do ensure that the pastry is cooked right through.

Take the *baklava* from the oven and pour the very cold syrup over the hot pastry. Leave to cool. When it is cold, cut into small diamonds and serve.

Baklava, the king of sweetmeats, has Turkish origins (top right). Basbousa (right) is one of many Middle Eastern sweetmeats made with semolina. It is ideal to serve at afternoon tea.

Basbousa with Coconut

100 g (4 oz) butter
150 g (5 oz) semolina
150 g (5 oz) sugar
75 g (3 oz) desiccated coconut
50 g (2 oz) plain flour
50 ml (2 fl oz) milk
1 teaspoon baking powder
vanilla extract
12 blanched almonds

Syrup
200 g (7 oz) sugar
1 tablespoon lemon juice
125 ml (4 fl oz) water, boiling

First make the syrup by dissolving the sugar and lemon juice in the water. Simmer until the syrup thickens, then remove it from the heat and allow to cool. Chill. Meanwhile, preheat the oven to 190°C/375°F/Gas 5.

To make the "cake", melt the butter and mix it with all the other ingredients in a large bowl. Stir well, then spoon into a shallow baking tray.

Bake about 30 minutes, or until golden. Remove from the oven and cut into diamond shapes placing an almond on each portion. Pour over half the syrup and bake a further 5 minutes until the *basbousa* are golden brown (be careful not to scorch the almonds).

Remove from the baking tray and serve warm with remaining syrup poured over them. Although *basbousa* are usually eaten warm, they are equally good chilled and will keep fresh for several days.

Ramadan Dessert

450 g (1 lb) dried apricots
225 g (8 oz) dried prunes
100 g (4 oz) sultanas
175 g (6 oz) raisins
4 chopped dried figs (optional)
600 ml (1 pint) water
50 g (2 oz) sugar
100 g (4 oz) mixed nuts (pine
* nuts, walnuts, almonds),*
* chopped*
single cream, to serve
grated nutmeg, to decorate

SERVES 6

Soak all the fruit overnight. Bring the water and sugar to the boil in a large saucepan. Stir 15–20 minutes, or until it becomes a syrupy consistency. Add all the fruits, mix together and simmer until soft but not breaking up. After 1 hour add the nuts and mix well.

Remove the mixture from the heat and allow to cool, then chill. Serve in a cut glass blowl or individual dishes. Pour single cream over the top and garnish with grated nutmeg.

Ramadan dessert is eaten when the Muslim fast is over at dusk.

Stuffed Dates

450 g (1 lb) fresh dates, stoned

Almond paste
100 g (4 oz) blanched almonds
1 large egg white
175 g (6 oz) icing sugar
2 teaspoons almond extract
2 drops rose water
green food colouring (optional)

MAKES 450 G (1 LB)

Preheat the oven to 160°C/325°F/Gas 3. Spread the almonds on a baking sheet and toast for 10 minutes, or until they are oily, but not brown. Cool, then grind in a food processor.

Add the egg white, sugar and almond extract, and process to give a firm paste. Add rose water, food colouring if using, and blend briefly. Chill overnight.

Open each date along the side it has been stoned and press a small amount of paste into each.

Almond Fingers

100 g (4 oz) unsalted butter
12 sheets filo pastry, thawed if
   frozen
50 g (2 oz) sugar
225 g (8 oz) ground almonds
pinch of ground cinnamon
1 teaspoon rose water
icing sugar

MAKES ABOUT 30

Melt the butter. Slice each sheet of pastry into 3 pieces. Brush each sheet with the melted butter. While doing this, preheat the oven to 160°C/325°F/Gas 3.

Mix together the sugar, ground almonds, cinnamon and rose water and spoon a portion across the centre of each filo sheet. Fold the sides in and roll into a neat cigar shape.

Place fingers in a row on a greased baking tray and brush the tops with remaining butter. Bake for about 40 minutes until pale golden, then remove and allow to cool. Sprinkle with the icing sugar.

Orange Slices with Cinnamon

3 oranges
ground cinnamon

SERVES 4

Choose navel oranges if possible. Peel and slice the oranges thinly, removing any pith and seeds. Arrange on a glass dish and sprinkle with ground cinnamon to taste. Chill, then remove from the refrigerator 10 minutes before serving.

Figs with Orange Juice

12 fresh figs
freshly squeezed juice of 6 oranges

SERVES 4

This is a simple dessert which can be prepared in advance. Cut the stalks off the fresh figs, but do not peel them. Quarter them and arrange in a flower effect on a dish. Cover with orange juice and chill.

Date and Banana Dessert

450 g (1 lb) fresh dates, stoned and halved
4 bananas
250 ml (8 fl oz) single cream
25 g (1 oz) roughly chopped walnuts
freshly grated nutmeg

SERVES 4

Fill either a glass bowl or individual glass dishes with alternate layers of halved dates and bananas. The dates should be as fresh as possible and should not be soft.

Cover with cream and chill for at least 2 hours so the dates will absorb the cream.

Garnish with walnuts and freshly grated nutmeg and serve.

These easy to prepare chilled desserts make an ideal end to a Middle Eastern meal: Figs with orange juice (top left); Orange slices with cinnamon (top right) and Date and banana dessert.

Hospitality is second nature in the Middle East. At the first sign of a visitor, coffee is put on the fire.

Drinks

Alcohol is forbidden by the *Quran*. This is not to say that several Middle Eastern countries do not produce some palatable wines: Turkey, Syria and Lebanon are wine producers and to a lesser extent, Egypt. The fiery aperitif *arak* is drunk in the Levant. The Turks drink it through the *mezze*, and, in fact, a *mezze* without *arak* (or *rakı*) is unthinkable.

Muslim families commonly drink mineral water or soft drinks with their meals. Lebanon bottles mineral water, and the tiny Gulf emirate of Ajman supplies the whole of Arabia with fine mineral water from an inland spring.

The ringing of the water seller's bell is still a familiar sound throughout the Middle East, particularly in Egypt. The bearer of news, the water seller has an important rank in street society. In the old days other street vendors used to sell fruit juices from glass flasks strapped onto their backs; today rows of juicers whizz in sidewalk cafés. Only in poor rural communities will you find someone still squeezing oranges, or pressing sugar cane on a crude machine salvaged from automobile parts.

Fresh lemon, or better still fresh lime juice, is my favourite cool drink on a hot day. In 1964, after travelling across North Africa, I spent some time staying with my cousin who worked at the British Embassy in Cairo. Each afternoon, an old lime seller used to call at her flat in Zamalek and on hearing his call from the street below, she would lower a basket for limes for our gin and tonics. And I particularly remember a tangy *limoonada* which revived me after a morning spent photographing the ruins of Persepolis, in Iran.

The ancient Persians were masters at making effervescent *sharbats* or sherbets from oranges, limes, apricots and other fruits. The pomegranate is a favourite fruit in Iran – it is said that the Prophet Muhammed urged his followers to eat it because it purged the system of envy and hatred. Using vivid metaphors, poets from Ferdowsi to the present day have compared the pomegranate to a woman's womb, ripe with progeny, to young maiden's cheeks and the opened fruit to a broken hearts, the seeds like tears of blood.

Tamarind juice is another popular beverage, especially in Syria and Iraq. The drink of nomads, yogurt and water, is commonly drunk with meals in Turkey and Yemen. Crushed almonds and milk is the stuff of the *Arabian Nights*.

Tea spiced with ginger and cinnamon is popular, but coffee, and the making and serving of coffee, has pride of place in Middle Eastern folklore, the whole coffee ritual being like a silent language that binds both host and guest.

In traditional Bedouin society, a guest is invited to take his place around the fire in the men's section of the tent. The host then digs into the coffee-bag and puts some beans in a ladle to roast on the embers. When they have cooled, he pounds them with a pestle and mortar or *mihbash* of traditional carved wood, or brass.

A skillful coffee grinder can pound out an appreciable rhythm audible at some distance, announcing to neighbours the arrival of a guest. The beans are tossed into boiling water and after boiling several times, the contents are poured into another pot and a pinch of freshly ground cardamom is added. This is allowed to simmer for about 15 minutes, the pleasant aroma pervading the whole tent.

The following gestures, now largely symbolic, remain essential protocol in the basic Bedouin coffee ceremony of the Middle East.

The first cup, offered to the host, is deemed the "unworthy cup", assuring the guest that the coffee is safe to drink and confirming to the host that it is hot, since it

is a terrible insult to serve cold coffee. Like the other cups, the second cup is poured with the left hand, the bearer palming the tiny white china cups in his right. This cup is offered to the guest whose acceptance signifies that he is pleased with the hospitality.

The third cup, even more significantly, has its roots in the days of tribal feuds. It silently concludes the protection agreement, meaning that the guest is safe from any attack while under the auspices of his host. This cup, known as the "sword cup", is binding, even against attack by one or the other's relatives. Sometimes a fourth cup is offered, confirming the silent defence pact.

It is not usual to drink more than this, but if a guest wants more (only a few drops are poured into each cup) he simply holds out his cup to be refilled by the attentive bearer. Alternatively, to signify he has had enough, he flicks the cup a couple of times with his wrist, the final concluding gesture to the coffee ritual.

Unfortunately, "Turkish coffee", as it is known in the West, is growing rare. High prices on the world coffee bean market have put many Middle Eastern coffee houses out of business, and in Mocha, the famous coffee port in Yemen, there is not even a drop of Nescafé! Chasing the quick profits from *qat*, local farmers have torn out their traditional coffee bushes and instead planted *Catha edulis* (*qat*).

Qahwa (Arabic for coffee) uses coffee grounds and cardamom pods in varying quantities. It is served at every opportunity. You can be seated only seconds in someone's home or office when, like a genie (or *djinn* in Arabic), a bearer arrives with a pot of *qahwa* and a stack of tiny cups.

On a royal tour of Saudi Arabia, as the only woman photographer, I often found myself *sans* men with the Queen in a harem. Emerging from a tent in Riyadh, about to step into her car, she was offered a cup of *qahwa*. Most of the time my presence was not acknowledged, but on this occasion her blue eyes glittered with humour: "This is my sixty-sixth cup of coffee since arriving in Arabia," she muttered, tossing it down like a Bedouin.

Yogurt Drink

900 ml (1¹/₂ pints) natural
   yogurt
1.25 litres (2¹/₄ pints) iced water
1 tablespoon finely chopped
   fresh mint
pinch of salt
fresh mint leaves, to garnish

SERVES 4

Mix all the ingredients together and pour into glasses, garnishing each with a little extra mint.

Using sparkling mineral water rather than iced water makes an even more refreshing drink. Serve well chilled.

Yogurt drink (above left) is especially popular in Iran and Turkey, while Almond drink echoes the Arabian Nights.

Almond Drink

150 g (5 oz) blanched almonds
sugar, to taste
350 ml (12 fl oz) water
600 ml (1 pint) milk
1 teaspoon orange blossom
   water
few drops of almond extract

SERVES 4

Chop the almonds and combine in a blender or food processor with the sugar and water. Blend until smooth, then add the remaining ingredients. Garnish each glass with a rose petal.

Middle Eastern Lemonade

8 lemons
150 g (5 oz) sugar, or to taste
1 teaspoon orange blossom
water, or to taste
generous 2 tablespoons freshly
chopped mint
still or sparkling water
ice cubes

SERVES 6

Squeeze the juice from the lemons and
sweeten to taste with sugar. Add the
orange blossom water and the mint, and
stir or shake well together. Pour a little
into a tall glass and fill with water and ice.

Orange Sharbat

16 medium oranges
sugar, to taste
1 teaspoon orange blossom
water
water and ice cubes
sprigs of fresh mint, to garnish

SERVES 6

Pomegranate Drink

Squeeze the juice from the oranges and sweeten to taste with sugar. Add the orange blossom water and mix well. Serve diluted with ice cold water and garnished with mint.

600 ml (1 pint) pomegranate juice
120 ml (4 fl oz) lemon juice
1 teaspoon orange blossom water
sugar, to taste
sparkling or still mineral water

SERVES 4–6

Combine everything in a blender, or mix well in a pitcher and serve with ice cubes.

Rose Petal Tea

rose petals from 4 roses
250 ml (8 fl oz) water
honey, to taste

SERVES 4

Choose fresh rose petals. Strip the flower gently under running water then place the petals in a saucepan. Cover with the water and boil for 5 minutes, or until the petals become discoloured. Strain into teacups and add honey to taste.

Qahwa   Arab coffee

6 cardamom pods
175 ml (6 fl oz) cold water
1 heaped tablespoon dark roast
*   coffee, coarsely ground*

SERVES 6

Bruise the cardamom pods by pounding gently in a pestle and mortar. Using a long-handled coffeepot (or a tiny saucepan), combine the water, pods and coffee. Bring to the boil, then simmer on a low heat for 15 minutes until the grounds settle.

Serve *qahwa* in tiny white coffee cups – Arabic ones do not have handles – about 2 tablespoons in each. *Qahwa* is not served with sugar, and its rather bitter flavour is not to everyone's taste. It is traditional Arabic coffee.

Turkish Coffee

2 tablespoons roasted ground
*   coffee*
1 heaped teaspoon sugar
3 small coffee cups water
tiny pinch of ground
*   cardamom*

SERVES 2

*There are three ways of ordering coffee in Arabic, and these are sweet (*helou *or* sukkar ziada*), medium (*mazbout*) or unsweetened (*murra*). Sugar is boiled with the coffee and the quantity will depend on the preference of your guests. This recipe is for medium coffee, to give an idea of the sugar quantities. If other guests require* helou *coffee, or no sugar at all, then you must brew another pot. Even if you like ordinary coffee without sugar, it is rare to drink Turkish coffee, as it is so sharp, without some sweetening.*

Combine all the ingredients in a long-handled coffeepot or tiny saucepan, stir well and bring to the boil. As the froth forms on top, remove from the stove, stir again and return to the heat until the froth rises again. Be very careful it does not boil over. Boil it briefly again, then stand aside for a few seconds.

Have the small cups ready to pour in the coffee, raising the pot (difficult with a saucepan) to get a nice head of froth on each cup. The grounds should be allowed to settle a minute or two before the coffee is drunk.

Turkish coffee (left), Rose petal tea (centre) and Qahwa *are common hot beverages in the Middle East. Turkish coffee is dark and strong, while* qahwa *is rather bitter.*

PAGES 148–149 *A lavish and generous end to a Middle Eastern meal. Freshly made* Baklava *(page 132) and* Almond Fingers *(page 137) are served with Turkish coffee, Turkish delight and fresh dates.*

147

Index

A

Almond drink *143*
Almond fingers *137*
Arabian cuisine *12–15*
Arab chopped salad *57*
Arab coffee *147*
Artichoke hearts in olive oil *33*
Asparagus salad *64*
Aubergine:
    Baked *69*
    Baked with cumin *70*
    Dip *25*
    Salad *60*

B

Babagannouj – aubergine dip *25*
Baked aubergine with cumin *70*
Baked aubergines *69*
Baked fish with saffron rice *84*
Baked squash in tahini sauce *75*
Baklava *132*
Banana and date dessert *138*
Banana loaf *130*
Barbecued fish with dates *87*
Basbousa with coconut *133*
Batata charp – stuffed potatoes *68*
Beid bi limoun – egg and lemon soup *48*
Beid ghanam – lambs' testicles *36*
Brains in lemon and olive oil *36*
Bread *7*
Broad bean patties *30*

C

Cabbage rolls *71*
"Caliph's delight" *128*
Carrot soup *45*
Casseroles:
    Chick pea and lamb *101*
    French bean *72*
    Lemon chicken *112*
    Okra and lamb *100*
    Persian with prunes *95*
    Turkish vegetable *76*
Chelo – Persian steamed rice *78*
Chick pea dip *26*
Chick pea and lamb casserole *101*

Chicken:
    Circassian chicken *115*
    Grilled lemon chicken *121*
    Hot chicken *116*
    Kebabs *120*
    Lemon chicken casserole *112*
    Musakhan chicken *114*
    Olives with chicken *122*
    Persian chicken *118*
    Roast, stuffed with rice and nuts   *119*
    Wings with garlic and yogurt *39*
    Yogurt and chicken *113*
Chilled cucumber and yogurt soup *45*
Coconut with basbousa *133*
Coffee:
    Turkish *147*
    Arab *147*
Cold fish in olive oil *82*
Courgette soup *53*
Courgettes with tomatoes *72*
Cucumber and raisin salad with yogurt *60*
Curry (prawn) *83*

D

Dates:
    Date and banana dessert *138*
    Dates with barbecued fish *87*
    Date *Ma'amoul* – date rolls *131*
    Date rolls *131*
    Stuffed dates *136*
Dietary laws *18*
Dolma – stuffed vine leaves *29*
Dried fruit salad *134*
Duck in walnut and pomegranate sauce
    123

E

Egg and lemon soup *48*
Egyptian cuisine *12*
Etiquette *18*

F

Falafel – broad bean patties *30*
Fattouche – mixed vegetable and bread
    salad *57*

Feast-day soup *51*
Ferakh al-hara – hot chicken *116*
Festivals *19*
Figs with orange juice *138*
Fish:
    Baked with saffron rice *86*
    Baked in *tahini* sauce *89*
    Barbecued with dates *87*
    Cold in olive oil *82*
    Fried *84*
    In hot sauce *88*
    Roe dip *26*
    Soup *49*
French bean stew *72*
French bean, leek and asparagus salad *65*
Fruit salad (dried) *134*

G

Green pepper salad *62*

H

Herb and nut omelette *74*
Hot pepper dip – *muhammara* *30*
Hummus – chick pea dip *26*

I

Imam bayildi *69*
Iraqi cuisine *17*

J

Jordanian cuisine *8–11*

K

Kadin Budu – "Lady's thighs" *24*
Kebabs:
    Chicken *120*
    Minced meat *106*
    Turkish style *107*

Kibbeh bi laban – meatballs *103*
Khoubz Arabieh – Pitta bread *41*
Kidney bean salad *57*
Kidneys in tomato sauce *109*

L

Labneh – thick yogurt *28*
"Lady's thighs" – *kabin budu 24*
Lamb:
    Braised chops and vegetables
        102
    and chick pea casserole *101*
    Levantine stew *94*
    and okra stew *100*
    Roast with yogurt and lemon
        99
    Roast stuffed with neck *96*
    Shoulder with saffron *98*
Lebanese cuisine, *8–11*
Lebanese "National" salad *32*
Leek salad *65*
Lemonade *144*
Lentil soup *51*
Levantine lamb stew *94*
Liver (fried) *36*

M

Meatballs *103*
Meatloaf (Syrian) *108*
Middle eastern lemonade *144*
Muhallabia – ground rice pudding *129*
Muhammara – hot pepper dip *30*
Mussels (fried) *39*

N

Nut and herb omelette *74*

O

Okra and lamb stew *100*
Okra stew *73*

Orange juice with figs *138*
Orange *sharbat 144*
Orange slices with cinnamon *138*

P

Pepper dip (hot) *30*
Persian casserole with prunes *95*
Persian cuisine *16–17*
Pickled chilli peppers *40*
Plain *pilau* rice *78*
Pomegranate drink *145*
Potato salad *62*
Potatoes (stuffed) *68*
Prawns in tomato sauce *85*

Q

Qahwa – Arab coffee *147*

R

Raisin and cucumber salad with yogurt *60*
Ramadan dessert *134*
Rice:
    Ground rice pudding *129*
    Persian steamed rice – *chelo 78*
    Plain *pilau* rice *78*
    Saffron rice *78*
Roast stuffed neck of lamb *96*
Rose petal tea *147*

S

Saffron rice *78*
Salata Arabieh – Arab chopped salad *57*
Salata fil-fil – sweet green pepper salad *62*
Sanbusak – stuffed crescent pastries *34, 35*
Sesame paste dip – *tahini 26*
Shoulder of lamb with saffron *98*
Spices *18–19*
Spinach pie *77*
Spinach salad *60*
Squid – stuffed *91*

Stuffed:
    Crescent pastries *34, 35*
    Potatoes *68*
    Tomatoes *68*
    Vine leaves *29*
Syrian cuisine *8–11*
Syrian meatloaf *108*
Syrian stuffed kibbeh *105*

T

Tabbouleh – Lebanese "National" salad *32*
Tahini – sesame paste dip *26*
Tahini sauce with baked fish *89*
Tahini sauce with baked aubergine *75*
Taramasalata – fish roe dip *26*
Thick yogurt *28*
Tomato:
    and coriander salad *62*
    sauce with kidneys *109*
    sauce with prawns *85*
    soup *44*
    stuffed *68*
Tuna *shashlik 90*
Turkish coffee *147*
Turkish cuisine *11*
Turkish-style kebabs *107*
Turkish vegetable casserole *76*

U

Umm Ali – "Mother of Ali" *127*

V

Vegetable and bread salad *57*
Vegetable casserole *76*
Vegetable and beef soup *52*
Vine leaves (stuffed) *29*

Y

Yemeni cuisine *15–16*

Acknowledgements

I would like to thank the following for their assistance with this book; Gulf Air, the national airline of Bahrain, Qatar and the Sultanate of Oman, which features Middle Eastern delicacies on its in-flight menu; Hilton Hotels Middle East and the Sheraton Hotels in Cairo and Sana'a. The Mena House Oberoi and the Khan el-Kalili Restaurant in Cairo were also very helpful, as were dozens of other small restaurants and local cooks who provided background information on food and cooking.

Christine Osborne

PICTURE CREDITS
Theo Bergström 14, 22–3, 24, 26–7, 28–9, 32–3, 34–5, 36–7, 38–9, 40–1, 44, 46–7, 49, 50–1, 52–3, 56–7, 58–9, 60–1, 62–3, 64–5, 68–9, 72–3, 74–5, 76–7, 78–9, 82–3, 84, 87, 88–9, 94, 96–7, 99, 100, 102–3, 104–5, 106, 108–9, 112, 114–5, 116–7, 118–9, 121, 122–3, 126–7, 128–9, 130, 132–3 top, 134–5, 137, 138–9, 142–3, 144–5, 146–7, 148–9

Michael Boys Syndication 15

COVER
Theo Bergström top 4 images, Christine Osborne bottom 3 images.

Christine Osborne/Middle Eastern Pictures title page, 4, 6, 9, 10, 13, 17, 18, 20, 30–1, 42, 54, 64, 80, 92, 110, 124, 140

Paris Graphic 25, 48, 70–1, 90–1, 98, 101, 107, 113, 120, 131, 133 bottom, 136

Prion Limited have endeavoured to observe the legal requirements with respect to suppliers of photographic material.